Foreword

The National Council on Ageing and Older People has long been concerned that older people are not overlooked in national and local development planning. At a time when preparations for a new seven-year development plan are beginning and when the Joint Ministerial Initiative on the Review of Local and Community Development Structures and Programmes is underway, the Council is pleased to present this study. It hopes that its conclusions and the Council Comments and Recommendations based on the findings will inform future local development planning and reviews of City/County Development Board strategies.

The social inclusion of older people at local level is the responsibility of all local government players, as well as older person's organisations and those working on behalf of older people. It is the responsibility of the Community and Voluntary Fora, Social Inclusion Measures Working Groups, local authority Strategic Policy Committees and all the constituent members of the City/County Development Boards. We hope that this study will be of assistance to them in carrying out their important work on behalf of their communities.

On behalf of the Council, I would like to thank Sarah Delaney, Kevin Cullen and Petrina Duff of the Work Research Centre for their commitment and dedication to the project. I would also like to thank Mr Pat O'Toole who chaired the Consultative Committee that assisted the progress of the research and oversaw the preparation of the report. Thanks are also due to the members of the Committee: Ms Kit Carolan; Cllr Jim Cousins; Ms Patricia Lane; Mr Pascal McDaid; Mr Pat McDonnell; Ms Shira Mehlman; Mr Kevin Molloy; Ms Mary Nally; Mr Michael O'Brien; Ms Sinead Pentony; Ms Mairead Ryan; Mr Eamonn Waters, Mr Colm Byrne; Mr David Silke. Finally, the Council would like to thank its Director, Mr Bob Carroll, and Research Officer, Ms Sinead Quill, who steered the project on the Council's behalf.

Eibhlin Byrne

Cllr Éibhlin Byrne
Chairperson

Authors' Acknowledgements

This report was commissioned by the National Council on Ageing and Older People (NCAOP). The Work Research Centre conducted the study. The study team comprised Mr Kevin Cullen (Study Coordinator and Centre Director), Ms Petrina Duff (Senior Research Consultant) and Ms Sarah Delaney (Research Consultant), with the assistance of Ms Marie Therese Fanning (Research Consultant).

We acknowledge the support and assistance of many individuals in completing this report. In particular, we would like to thank the representatives of the County and City Development Boards and associated structures, and the representatives of older people in the 34 CDB areas for participating in the research and for making such a valuable contribution. We also extend our thanks to the members of the Consultative Committee for the study: Ms Kit Carolan; Cllr Jim Cousins; Ms Patricia Lane; Mr Pascal McDaid; Mr Pat McDonnell; Ms Shira Mehlman; Mr Kevin Molloy; Ms Mary Nally; Mr Michael O'Brien; Mr Pat O'Toole (Chair); Ms Sinead Pentony; Ms Mairead Ryan; Mr Eamonn Waters, Mr Colm Byrne and Mr David Silke for their guidance and support throughout the research. We would especially like to thank Mr Bob Carroll (Director), Ms Sinead Quill (Research Officer) and Ms Liza Costello (Research Assistant) of the NCAOP for their hard work and support throughout the research process.

The Social Inclusion of Older People at Local Level

The Role and Contribution of CDBs

Sarah Delaney, Kevin Cullen and Petrina Duff
Work Research Centre

National Council on Ageing and Older People

Report no. 90

', 16992 91 X

National Council on Ageing and Older People
22 Clanwilliam Square
Grand Canal Quay
Dublin 2

Report no. 90
© National Council on Ageing and Older People, 2005
ISBN 1 900378 36 1
Price: €14

Cover image kindly provided by West Cork Arts Centre in association with
Skibbereen Day Care Centre.

Contents

List of Tables

List of Figures

Council Comments and Recommendations

Council Comments and Recommendations

Background

The Council has consistently advocated greater coordination and integration of services for older people at local, regional and national levels. It considers that 'the needs of older people cannot be accommodated in watertight compartments' and 'rigid boundaries between Government Departments, providing agencies, professionals and service users themselves, frequently are harmful to older people's interests' (Browne, 1992). As far back as 1985, the Council outlined its perspective on the issue of service coordination in the reports *Housing of the Elderly in Ireland* (NCE, 1985a) and *Institutional Care of the Elderly in Ireland* (NCE, 1985b). Building on these reports, the Council proposed the establishment of two pilot projects on the coordination of services for older people to test certain aspects of the model outlined in its reports. These pilot projects, which ran from 1987 to 1991 in Dun Laoghaire and Tipperary S.R., are the subject of the evaluation report *Coordinating Services for the Elderly at Local Level: Swimming Against the Tide* (Browne, 1992).

The Council has also long been committed to assisting in improving the social inclusion of older people at all levels of Irish society (*Towards a Society for All Ages*, 2001; *An Age Friendly Society: A Position Statement*, 2005). In this context, it recently observed that 'an age friendly society in Ireland will encourage the full participation and integration of all older people in our society' and '... the effectiveness of our policies and practices will be judged on the basis of how well they meet the needs of our older population' (NCAOP, 2005).

It is against the background of previous Council research and considered Council opinion that the current study is set.

Defining Social Inclusion

As highlighted in the report, social inclusion is a complex concept that is difficult to define and quantify. Typically, objective indicators of social exclusion, such as poverty and unemployment, are measured when establishing the social inclusion or exclusion of a particular societal group. This is primarily because positive indicators of social inclusion, for example participation and social integration, are ephemeral and more difficult to quantify. In this regard, the 2004 Survey on Income and Living Conditions (CSO, 2005) confirmed that older people are vulnerable to both poverty and social exclusion, with 7 per cent of older people living in consistent poverty and more than one third (36.4 per cent) at risk of poverty, compared with 22 per cent of the rest of the population[1].

Three definitions relating to social inclusion appear in Government policy documents. The National Anti-Poverty Strategy (NAPS) definition of poverty states that 'people are living in poverty if their income and resources (material, cultural and social) are so inadequate as to preclude them from having a standard of living which is regarded as acceptable by Irish society generally. As a result of inadequate income and resources, people may be excluded and marginalised from participating in activities which are considered the norm for other people in society' (Government of Ireland, 1997). *Partnership 2000* (Department of the Taoiseach, 1998) asserts that social exclusion results in cumulative marginalisation from production, consumption, social networks, decision-making and from an adequate quality of life, while *Sustaining Progress* (Department of the Taoiseach, 2003) states that in an inclusive society 'people have the resources and opportunities to live life with dignity and have access to the quality public services that underpin life chances and experiences'. Some commonalities between these definitions can be identified, such as preclusion from an adequate quality of life and marginalisation from the rest of society. The definition of poverty, however, differs from those of social exclusion by placing a stronger focus on the causal effect of inadequate income.

The present study found that when translating national social inclusion commitments to a local level, some County and City Development Boards (CDBs) are using the Partnership 2000 definition, others are using the NAPS definition, while others have developed their own definitions. Research has highlighted that the relationship between income and experience of exclusion is less evident among older people than it is for the rest of the population (O'Reilly, 2002). In order to ensure inclusion of older people in social inclusion measures, the Council therefore advocates that CDB operations should be guided by a definition of social exclusion, rather than one of poverty.

1 Social transfers are not taken into account in this translation.

About the CDBs

The CDBs were established in 2000 with the aim of bringing about more coordinated delivery of public and local development services. They mark a significant stage in the history of community development and subsidiarity in Ireland. Membership is drawn from each region's local authority, State agencies, local development bodies and social partners. Social inclusion is an important aspect of the work of the CDBs. This is reflected in the establishment of Social Inclusion Measures Working Groups (SIMs), whose brief is to coordinate the local delivery of the social inclusion components of the National Development Plan (NDP) 2000-2006 (Department of Finance, 1999), as well as broadening their scope to address wider social inclusion issues.

In January 2005, each CDB was asked to carry out a review of its strategy for economic, social and cultural development. The review is focusing on the CDBs' core coordination roles and should result in:

■ the selection of a limited number of key priorities and actions on which each CDB will concentrate over the following three years

■ a focus on integrative actions aimed at a more joined-up approach to local service delivery involving relevant agencies.

It is not envisaged that the review will result in fundamental changes to the overall strategy. However, it is likely that some adjustments, refinement and rebalancing of priorities and implementation arrangements will be proposed in the light of developments and experience to date. When complete, the review will provide detail on progress in the implementation of the strategies and social inclusion measures. The Council considers that this research is both timely and relevant to this stage of evolution of the CDB process and it is hoped that this report will be of assistance in informing the review and its conclusions.

Recommendations

While this study focused on CDBs to identify social inclusion measures for older people at local level, it is important to recognise that the ultimate function of CDBs is to act as a coordinating body for existing organisations and agencies.

Responsibility for the inclusion of older people in the development of social inclusion measures at local level lies not only with the CDBs, but also with the agencies represented on them, as well as older people's representative organisations and the community and voluntary sector as a whole.

The researchers identified three main themes during the course of the study, around which they made a series of recommendations for action (see Chapter Six). In keeping with the report, the Council has organised its recommendations under the same themes, which are as follows:

- including older people in local level planning and decision-making

- addressing older people's concerns in a comprehensive manner

- the roles of other national and local agencies.

The Council's recommendations are grounded in the findings of this study and it is hoped that their implementation will play an important role in combating social exclusion experienced by many older people, and in promoting the social inclusion of older people in local development processes.

Including Older People in Local Level Planning and Decision-Making

Raising Awareness

In *An Age Friendly Society: A Position Statement*, the Council highlighted the need to promote an anti-ageist philosophy at all levels of our society (NCAOP, 2005). It believes that this is necessary to combat endemic ageism and promote the inclusion of older people in national, regional and local decision-making processes, including how services are developed, structured and delivered.

In this regard, the Council recognises the valuable contribution the Age and Opportunity Agewise equality training programme makes in enabling participants to:

- understand the personal, cultural and structural effects of ageism

- identify instances of discrimination against older people

- devise strategies to counter age discrimination in their workplace or community.

The Council recommends that this and other like initiatives should be supported and developed. It is particularly concerned to promote training for an age friendly society, leading to a better understanding of ageing and older people in all walks of life and particularly in fora where decisions affecting the welfare of older people are taken. Building on its wealth of research and information on ageing and older people, the Council will endeavour to support the development of a more comprehensive programme of training for an age friendly society in partnership with other agencies.

Consultation with Older People

In recent years, the Council has emphasised the importance of meaningful consultation with older people regarding their needs and preferences. This research study found that while many older people wish to become involved in local development processes, others have a greater concern to access community services. For this reason, effective models and guidelines on consultation with older people are vital, to assist those who wish to become involved in decision-making processes and to ensure that the views of those who are not involved are taken into account. In this context, the Council reiterates the recommendation it made in its *HeSSOP* report 'that a democratic approach to consultation is the way forward'. Such an approach ensures that 'governing bodies ... yield some of the power they hold to consumers' and it allows consumers to 'take an active role in the decision-making process, including how services are developed, structured and delivered' (Garavan *et al.*, 2001).

In this regard, the Council welcomes the preparation of guidelines on customer consultation by the Local Government Customer Service Group, which will advise local authorities on mechanisms for consulting with the public in relation to the delivery of services.

In addition, the Council recommends that CDBs and their member organisations should incorporate consultation with older people in the development of any plan of work that relates to them or whose output affects them.

Capacity-building

As noted in the research report, social inclusion initiatives are as much about the process of decision-making as about tangible outcomes for target groups. Current membership of the CDBs is necessarily prescriptive, not only to avoid them becoming large and unwieldy, but also to ensure that membership is as balanced as possible. This structure is not expected to change as a result of the current review. It appears that the principal means of representation of older people and their representative groups will remain via the Community and Voluntary Fora

16

that operate in each of the CDB areas. To increase the influence of older people in all development processes and in all relevant local agencies, it is necessary to consider the issue of capacity-building among older people's organisations and representative groups.

In this regard, the Council welcomes the recent ADM report on a community development approach to working with older people (ADM, 2005), and recommends that this approach should become integral to the work of older people's interest groups and to the manner in which relevant agencies engage with older people[2]. This would greatly facilitate the inclusion of older people's perspectives in the planning, policy and decision-making processes that significantly affect their lives.

Addressing Older People's Concerns in a Comprehensive Manner

Council research has consistently drawn attention to the heterogeneity of the older population, and emphasised the diversity of their needs, preferences and experiences (NCAOP, 2005). In this regard, a significant finding of this study was that the range of support and services provided to the older population varied across the CDBs. For example, issues such as employment, accessible public places, gender and income tended to be given less consideration than others.

Consultation with older people's representative organisations in the course of the study highlighted the need for a dedicated worker for older people. The role of such a worker would incorporate information provision, advocacy, organising and coordinating initiatives, and promoting inter-agency coordination. Such a worker would facilitate the coming together of older persons' organisations and organisations working on behalf of older persons, so that they can take responsibility for formulating common positions on issues affecting them locally. To be successful in this role, it is therefore likely that the dedicated worker will not be affiliated to any of the organisations concerned. As an advocate working on behalf of all older persons, the dedicated worker will also be independent of local authorities and decision-makers.

While, acknowledging the important role currently played by Community and Enterprise Development Officers (CEDOs) and other local development agencies, the Council recommends the piloting of a programme of dedicated workers for older people in a number of local areas. The Council would be pleased to assist in the identification of current best practice in this regard and in the initiation of such a project.

2   The report defines the community development approach as 'enabling socially excluded people to work together in shaping the emergence of a more just society, through collectively identifying and tackling inequalities and influencing the conditions which affect their everyday lives.'

As observed by the Council in *Coordinating Services for the Elderly at Local Level: Swimming Against the Tide*, there are 'several levels at which coordination must be activated ranging from the national level to the local district, and different tasks will be appropriate to certain levels and not to others' (Browne, 1992).

This research report suggests that older people's interests are still suffering from limited coordination. In general, it was found that local agencies tended to confine their activities within existing structures and boundaries, with little evidence of any meaningful coordination. This can lead to failure in addressing gaps in social inclusion measures for older people. It also found a complex linkage between the various national and local agencies, caused primarily by the sheer number of relevant parties, which was partly attributed to problems in achieving integration among agencies. **In this regard, the Council welcomes the recommendation arising from the recent IPA review of Strategic Policy Committees (SPCs) concerning coordination and cohesion between SPCs and CDBs, which advocates the need for improved linkages and information-sharing.**

18

A further crucial element of coordination, in a vertical context, relates to policy documents developed at a national level. These inform and direct the development of CDB strategic and operational plans, and affect both the level of coordination between agencies as well as consideration of the needs and experiences of older people in service planning. In order to ensure that older people are protected against any inequalities at national policy level, **the Council recommends that Government age proof its policies and that this is mirrored in the development of CDB strategies and plans, in order to ensure that the needs of older people are accommodated at local, regional and national levels.**

Finally, coordination at a national level between Government Departments is a prerequisite for coordination at a local level. The findings of this research study show that without improved coordination at national level, efforts to promote coordination at local level will be 'swimming against the tide'. **In this regard, the Council welcomes the NESF recommendation that a Government agreement be put in place on required joint collaboration and a Department nominated as a lead agency. The Council also welcomes the establishment of the Inter-Departmental Group on Older People (IDGOP) in 2003 as a first and necessary step in coordinating departmental activities to the benefit of older people and it recommends that the IDGOP continue to develop its programme of work, which has the potential to play a significant role in encouraging an ethos of coordination at all levels.**

Conclusion

In the Madrid International Plan of Action on Ageing (UN, 2002), the United Nations (UN) states that a political, economic, ethical and spiritual view for the social development of older persons is required to respond to the opportunities and challenges of population ageing in the twenty-first century and to promote the development of a society for all ages. The Plan emphasises that a necessary first step in this regard is to mainstream ageing and the concerns of older people into national development frameworks and poverty eradication strategies.

In this context, the Council advocates including ageing and the concerns of older people in the social partnership process. In its position statement, *An Age Friendly Society* (NCAOP, 2005), it is stated that 'there is an urgent need to develop a national coordinated strategy on ageing and older people to ensure the full implementation of UN, WHO and national aspirations for the participation, security and health of older people in our society'.

In the context of the current study, the Council would emphasise that all local areas should also develop coordinated strategies on ageing and older people with a similar aim of promoting the participation, security and health of older people at local level. To achieve this, ageing and the concerns of older people must also be mainstreamed in all local development strategies.

Area Development Management Ltd, 2005. *Age and Change: A Community Development Approach to Working with Older People*. Dublin: ADM Ltd.

Browne, M., 1992. *Coordinating Services for the Elderly at Local Level: Swimming Against the Tide*. Dublin: NCE.

Central Statistics Office, 2005. *EU Survey on Income and Living Conditions (EU-SILC): First Results*. Dublin: Stationery Office.

Department of Finance, 1999. *National Development Plan, 2000-2006*. Dublin: Stationery Office.

Department of the Taoiseach, 1998. *Partnership 2000*. Dublin: Stationery Office.

Department of the Taoiseach, 2003. *Sustaining Progress*. Dublin: Stationery Office.

Garavan, R., Winder, R. and McGee, H., 2001. *Health and Social Services for Older People (HeSSOP)*. Dublin: NCAOP.

Government of Ireland, 1997. *National Anti-Poverty Strategy*. Dublin: Stationery Office.

McGivern, Y., 2001. *Towards a Society for All Ages*. Dublin: NCAOP.

National Council for the Elderly, 1985a. *Housing for the Elderly in Ireland*. Dublin: NCE.

National Council for the Elderly, 1985b. *Institutional Care of the Elderly in Ireland*. Dublin: NCE.

National Council on Ageing and Older People, 2005. *An Age Friendly Society: A Position Statement*. Dublin: NCAOP.

O'Reilly, D., 2002. 'Standard indicators of deprivation: do they disadvantage older people?' *Age and Ageing*, 31: 197-202.

United Nations, 2002. *Madrid International Plan of Action on Ageing*. New York: UN.

20

Executive Summary

Executive Summary

Introduction

The National Council on Ageing and Older People (NCAOP) commissioned the Work Research Centre (WRC) to investigate the social inclusion measures for older people being undertaken at local level in Ireland and to examine the role and contribution of the County/City Development Boards (CDBs) in the social inclusion of older people at local level. The CDBs were targeted because of the pivotal role that they have been given in local development processes.

About the CDBs

The CDBs were established in 2000 to bring about more coordinated delivery of public and local development services at local level. Their membership is drawn from local authorities, the social partners, State agencies operating locally and local development organisations. CDB members are nominated in line with guidelines published by the Department of the Environment, Heritage and Local Government (DoEHLG) in 1999. A core function of the CDBs was to draw up and oversee the implementation of a ten-year strategy for the economic, social and cultural development of their areas. These strategies were published in 2002.

The strategies are delivered by the member agencies of the CDBs, each of which delivers elements through their operational plans and services for the area. Responsibility for achieving an action is allocated to a nominated lead agency. These agencies are required to develop a work plan based on the strategic actions and issues identified in the strategies.

Social inclusion is an important aspect of the remit of the CDBs and, in practice, social inclusion related activities form a substantial part of their work. In addition, a Social Inclusion Measures Working Group (SIM) was set up by each CDB to coordinate the local delivery of the social inclusion components of the National Development Plan (NDP) and to address wider social inclusion issues.

Community and Voluntary Fora were established in each of the CDB areas. These Fora have two key roles: to act as a platform for community and voluntary groups to participate in matters relating to the CDBs; and to provide a structure through which community and voluntary representatives can participate in the CDBs.

About the Study

Aims and Objectives

The central focus of the research was to identify the operations of and concrete measures that are being planned or implemented at local level by the 34 CDBs, via their member agencies, in the development and implementation of social inclusion measures for older people.

The specific objectives of the study were:

- to ascertain how the operations and priority areas of CDBs are determined

- to ascertain the degree of input of older people and the organisations that represent them into the CDBs

- to assess the work of the CDBs in the promotion of the social inclusion of older people

- to investigate the terms of reference of the CDBs and associated bodies, such as the SIMs, the composition of these groups, and the operations and priority areas of these groups

- to detail the measures that are being planned or undertaken at local level to promote the social inclusion of older people

- to identify the gaps in such measures and the additional measures required to facilitate greater inclusion and participation by older people in CDBs and in Irish society

- to explore whether the actions taken are consistent with national priority areas (e.g. work and retirement, lifelong learning, income, transport, housing, health and community services) with regard to older people and to comment in this regard.

Methodology

The research was conducted in four stages:

- primary data gathering incorporating document collation and processing, interviews with representatives from the 34 CDBs and semi-structured interviews with older people or their representatives from 25 CDB areas

- interview analysis incorporating quantitative and qualitative analysis of the primary data generated from the CDB strategy documents and the interviews with local actors

- contextual analysis and literature reviewing

- synthesis of research and reporting.

Conclusions

The conclusions that are drawn from the research and the associated recommended actions focus on the following:

- the role and contribution of the CDBs to the social inclusion of older people at local level, and the scope for extension and improvement in this area

- the role and contribution of other local and national agencies to the social inclusion of older people at local level.

This analysis is timely given that the CDBs have been in operation for a number of years. In addition, there have been a number of developments that suggest that this is an opportune time to seek to promote the social inclusion agenda for older people at local level via the CDBs and associated local processes, such as the SIMs and the Community and Voluntary Fora. These will help to put in place mechanisms to improve the consistency of approach to social inclusion issues by the CDBs and SIMs, and to enhance the reach and effectiveness of the Community and Voluntary Fora. They provide a genuine opportunity for ensuring the concerns of older people are placed on the local development agenda.

The recommended actions have been proposed on the basis of the research findings and conclusions. In all cases, such actions should seek to build on existing work of relevance, including work by the NCAOP, Equality Authority and other key agencies.

The Role of CDBs in the Social Inclusion of Older People

The CDBs were established to fulfil a central role in local government policy in Ireland and have the potential to make a significant contribution to the promotion of social inclusion of older people at local level. Key mechanisms for achieving this include:

■ including older people and older people's representative organisations in local level planning and decision-making

■ addressing older people's concerns in a comprehensive manner in CDB strategies and the programmes of action to implement the strategies.

Inclusion of Older People in Local Level Planning and Decision-Making

Social inclusion initiatives are as much about the process of decision-making as about tangible outcomes for target groups. Therefore, the involvement of older people should in itself be part of the social inclusion process. In addition, older people themselves are best able to identify their own needs and how they should be met.

Recommended Actions

1. An awareness-raising programme should be launched to promote positive attitudes towards ageing and older people at local level. This should target the CDBs and their member agencies, as well as those involved in related local structures such as the Community and Voluntary Fora.

2. The measures recently implemented to develop and reinforce the role of the Community and Voluntary Fora provide an opportunity for a nationwide effort to increase the representation and influence of older people in local development processes across Ireland including to raise awareness of the need to involve older people and their representative organisations and to provide guidance on good practice in consulting and involving older people, taking into account the recommendations of the review of the Community and Voluntary Fora carried out in 2004.

3. A programme focusing on capacity-building among older people's organisations at local level could be developed with a view to ensuring that they are equipped to avail of the opportunities for participation that are emerging. This might begin on a pilot basis, working with older people and their organisations in one or more local areas. A detailed audit of existing levels of organisation, capacities and extent of involvement in local processes could be carried out, followed by the design and implementation of an intervention to address barriers to effective involvement and influence. Based on the results of the pilot intervention, a wider programme of intervention could then be developed across the country.

Addressing Older People's Concerns in a Comprehensive Manner

In addition to involving older people and older people's organisations in decision-making, the social inclusion of older people at local level can also be promoted by:

- giving a high priority to older people in CDB strategies, backed up by a comprehensive range of measures to address older people's concerns and the gaps in service provision identified by older people and their representative organisations

- developing the degree of inter-agency coordination needed to provide joined-up services and supports for older people.

Our analysis of CDB strategies identified a wide range of practical measures focusing on the needs of older people. Looking at the range of specific services and supports for older people that are planned in the CDB strategies, it was found that more attention is currently being given at local level to some of the national policy priority areas for older people, such as housing and health and community services, than to others, such as employment, accessible public places, gender and income.

Recommended Actions

4. It is recommended that guidance documentation be prepared and distributed to the CDBs on the concerns of older people and how these can be addressed at local level. One way to progress this might be to seek to work in the first instance, on a pilot basis, with a limited number of CDBs in order to explore the most appropriate approaches before launching a countrywide initiative. The guidance documentation could delineate the issues that need to be addressed to meet the range of concerns of older people, as well as indicating the ways that the various issues could be addressed at local level. This could include measures addressing at-risk older people, issues that apply across the population (recognition, status, equality/anti-discrimination, socially valued roles etc.) and specific themes that are important for many older people (e.g. health and social services, active retirement, social participation). In this regard, it should be noted that perspectives on social inclusion that focus mainly on income and unemployment dimensions do not always capture other aspects of social inclusion and exclusion that are particularly relevant for older people.

A number of key gaps in service provision were also identified in interviews carried out with older people's representative organisations. These focused on the need to expand choice, mainstream existing initiatives and improve linkages between discrete services. It is important to take account of these needs in future planning. The fact that interviewees also recommended the introduction of dedicated workers for older people is of note. This should be progressed in consultation with older people and their representative organisations.

Recommended Actions

5. The gaps in service provision identified by older people's organisations should be noted and actions developed to address these. With regard to dedicated workers for older people, a pilot project utilising international best practice could be developed, in partnership with older people and their representative organisations, to explore the cost implications, responsibilities and job description of such a worker.

In addition to the direct measures proposed in their strategies, the CDBs play a central role in the coordination of services and the activities of their member agencies. This is an ongoing aspect of the operations of the CDBs, as well as being reflected in various ways in the CDB strategy documents. This study found that although coordination type measures and approaches addressing issues of relevance for older people were to be found in the majority of CDB strategies, there was considerable diversity in the way that the coordination issue was addressed.

Recommended Actions

6. It is recommended that an analysis be carried out of the key inter-agency issues that are most pertinent to the concerns of older people at local level. This would examine whether there are gaps in service provision that arise because of a lack of coordination across organisational boundaries. Transport and education are just two of the areas where there is a need for much greater coordination of services for older people. This should take account of the gaps identified by older people's organisations during the course of the current study.

The Roles and Contribution of Other National and Local Agencies

Although the CDBs have considerable potential for delivering on social inclusion for older people at local level in Ireland, it would be inappropriate to place all of the responsibility for this area on them. Other players at both local and national levels must contribute.

National Level

Reviews of CDB activities and achievements have indicated that many of the inter-agency coordination objectives that have been set for the local level cannot be realised without commensurate inter-Departmental and inter-agency coordination at national level. For this reason, it is necessary to have national level coordination across Government Departments and agencies with roles to play in the social inclusion of older people if a coordinated approach is to be achieved at local level.

Recommended Actions

7. With regard to inter-Departmental and inter-agency coordination at national level, there is a need for a parallel analysis and programme of action to that suggested for local level. This is something that might fall directly within the remit of the Interdepartmental Group on Older People (IDGOP).

The CDBs were established to provide a locally driven approach to identifying priority local development issues and preparing strategies to address these. Clearly, therefore, principles of subsidiarity must be applied when considering what role should be played at national level in relation to ensuring consistency of approach across the country. Nevertheless, Government Departments and public agencies at national level have a responsibility to ensure a basic level and quality of services for older people in all parts of the country.

Recommended Actions

8. With regard to ensuring a basic level and quality of services for older people across the country, various Government Departments and national agencies have roles to play in defining and implementing minimum standards. The DoHC and the HSE, in particular, could address the issue of consistent provision and access to services for older people across the country.

Local Level

In addition to the CDBs and their member agencies, there are many local agencies and programmes with roles to play in the delivery of social inclusion measures for older people.

9. The awareness-raising and guidance activities proposed earlier for the CDBs could also be targeted towards these other local level agencies and activities.

Chapter One

Introduction

Chapter One
Introduction

1.1 Introduction

This report documents a study to investigate the social inclusion measures for older people being undertaken at local level in Ireland and examine the role and contribution of the County and City Development Boards (CDBs) in the social inclusion of older people at local level. It was expected that the results would help the NCAOP:

- to ascertain the visibility of older people on the local social inclusion agenda

- to identify areas where additional supports are required to facilitate greater inclusion and participation by older people in Irish society

- to advise at regional level in addition to its usual practice of advising at national level.

In seeking to gather information and analyse local level activity in support of older people, the research focused on the role the 34 CDBs play in relation to the coordination and implementation of all publicly funded activities, including those relating to social inclusion at local level. The fact that each CDB was required to establish a local Social Inclusion Measures Working Group (SIM) to inform a social inclusion strategy for each city/county indicates the key role envisaged for the CDBs in relation to social inclusion and suggested that it was appropriate to investigate the role and contribution CDBs make to the social inclusion measures of older people at local level.

1.2.1 About the CDBs

The Interdepartmental Task Force on the Integration of Local Government and Local Development Systems identified the need for the establishment of a CDB in each of the 34 local authority areas. The Task Force envisaged that the establishment of the CDBs:

■ would provide a greater sense of ownership and commitment, initially across the Board membership and thereafter throughout the county

■ would reinvigorate local governance through effective local integration of public services leading to a better quality of life for all citizens.

The CDBs were established in 2000 and their primary functions were defined under Section 129 of the Local Government Act, 2001. These were:

■ to take such steps as the Board may consider appropriate to enable each of the bodies and interests whose functions affect the social, economic or cultural development of the county or city or any part of the county or city and its people to provide the maximum each of them can to such development, both individually and collectively

■ to draw up a strategy for the social, economic and cultural development of the county or city and the community

■ to seek to secure that the policies and operations of the bodies and interests represented on the Board and of others accord generally with the strategy

■ to encourage and promote on an ongoing basis the coordination of activities of the bodies and interests represented on the Board and cooperation generally between such bodies and interests so as to optimise resources and combined effort for the common good of the community.

A key role of the CDBs was to prepare a ten-year social, economic and cultural strategy for their county or city. Since the publication of these strategies in 2002, a number of developments have taken place. Both the strategy development process and the impact of these developments on the work of the CDBs will be discussed in more detail in Chapter Five.

1.2.2 Social Inclusion Policy

At Irish and European levels the theme of social inclusion has come to the fore as the focal point for much social policy.

1.2.2.1 The National Anti-Poverty Strategies (NAPS and Revised NAPS)

The main vehicles specifically designed to address social inclusion in Ireland are the National Anti-Poverty Strategy (NAPS) and Revised National Anti-Poverty Strategy (Revised NAPS). The first NAPS was launched in 1997 and was coordinated by the NAPS unit of the Department of Social, Community and Family Affairs (DoSCFA). The Revised NAPS was published in 2002, and provided a framework for tackling poverty and social exclusion. Older people were one of the vulnerable groups identified for particular attention in Revised NAPS.

Definitions of social inclusion and social exclusion were not set out in either strategy. However, the definition of poverty set out in both strategies was later adopted by the CDBs in relation to their social inclusion work, as well as by later NAPS/Inclusion strategies.

1.2.2.2 The National Development Plan (NDP)

The promotion of social inclusion is one of the four key national objectives in the National Development Plan (NDP). The definition of social inclusion included in the Plan was taken from the Partnership 2000 agreement, in which social exclusion was defined as 'cumulative marginalisation: from production (unemployment), from consumption (income poverty), from social networks (community, family and neighbours), from decision-making and from an adequate quality of life' (Department of the Taoiseach, 1997). The CDBs, through their SIMs, were identified as the vehicle for the delivery of social inclusion objectives at local level.

1.3 Aims and Objectives of the Research

The specific aims of the research were to identify the operations of and concrete measures that are being planned or implemented at local level by the CDBs in the development and actualisation of social inclusion measures for older people as detailed in the CDB strategies. Against this background, the specific objectives of the study were as follows:

- to ascertain how the operations and priority areas of CDBs are determined

- to ascertain the degree of input of older people and the organisations that represent them into the CDBs

- to assess the work of the CDBs in the promotion of the social inclusion of older people

- to investigate the terms of reference of the CDBs and associated bodies, such as the SIMs, the composition of these groups, and the operations and priority areas of these groups

- to detail the measures that are being planned or undertaken at local level to promote the social inclusion of older people

- to identify the gaps in such measures and the additional measures required to facilitate greater inclusion and participation by older people in CDBs and in Irish society

- to explore whether the actions taken are consistent with national priority areas (e.g. work and retirement, lifelong learning, income, transport, housing, health and community services) with regard to older people and to comment in this regard.

1.4 Methodology

The research was conducted in four stages:

- primary data gathering

- interview analysis

- contextual analysis and literature review

- synthesis and reporting.

1.4.1 Primary Data Gathering

The principal elements of this stage of the process were document collation and processing; interviews with CDB representatives; and liaison and consultation with older people and their representatives at local level.

1.4.1.1 Document Collation and Processing

This involved collating and processing available documentation on each of the CDBs, including strategy documents, implementation plans and reports, in order to analyse the specifics of each CDB and its documented plans and activities in relation to older people.

1.4.1.2 Interviews with CDB Representatives

In consultation with the NCAOP, the Community and Enterprise Development Officers (CEDOs) of the local authorities were selected as the group most appropriate to interview, as they were identified as individuals who would be sufficiently informed about the CDB's *modus operandi* and substantive activities. In total, interviews with CEDOs were held in 27 of the 34 CDB areas. Where access to a CEDO could not be arranged, interviews were held with SIM members (four CDB areas) and with Directors of Community and Enterprise (four CDB areas). In one county, interviews were carried out with both a CEDO and a SIM member.

Most of the interviews were carried out on a face-to-face basis. In a minority of cases where a face-to-face meeting could not be arranged, telephone interviews were held instead. Interviews were successfully completed with representatives of all 34 CDBs. The protocol used for these interviews is included in Appendix One.

1.4.1.3 Liaison and Consultation with Older People and Their Representatives

Efforts were also made to engage in liaison and consultation with older people and their representative organisations at local level, in order to assess their levels of satisfaction in relation to the CDBs. The principal method used was face-to-face, semi-structured interviews. The sample was generated through contacts provided by CDB representatives as well as information on active local organisations from the NCAOP and other central sources. It sometimes proved very difficult to identify suitable respondents to interview, often because local organisations for older people are quite far removed from CDB structures and processes. Nevertheless it proved possible to carry out interviews with older people's representatives in 25 CDB areas. The protocol used for these interviews is included in Appendix One.

1.4.2 Interview Analysis

A combination of qualitative and quantitative analysis was carried out on the primary data generated from the CDB strategy documents and the interviews with local actors.

A template was prepared for extraction of the main aspects of each CDB's activities in relation to older people. This was systematically applied to the documentation available from each CDB in order to prepare profiles of each of the 34 CDBs. In addition, basic tabulations of key aspects were prepared in order to provide some quantitative indications of the frequency of occurrence and/or spread across CDBs of some of the issues of interest.

The information from the interviews with local actors was coded and analysed using the NUD*IST qualitative data analysis package. This enabled the compilation of basic tabulations and the extraction of core qualitative themes from the interviews.

1.4.3 Contextual Analysis and Literature Review

Another important element of the research involved contextual analysis of the structural and policy dimensions of the themes of interest to the study. This included examinations of:

- the general role and structure of the CDBs and associated entities, such as SIMs
- the European, national and local contexts for social inclusion policy and practice
- the theoretical and empirical literature relating to social inclusion and older people
- Irish policy priorities regarding the concerns of older people.

1.4.4 Synthesis and Reporting

Finally, the various elements of the research were synthesised and drawn upon in order to make an overall assessment of the extent to which the CDBs are addressing the concerns of older people in their social inclusion processes. This provided the basis for the formulation of recommendations on how attention to the concerns of older people could be further developed at local level in Ireland.

1.5 Structure of the Report

The report is structured in five chapters as follows. Chapter Two examines the concept of social inclusion and how it is applied in policy and practice at European, national and local levels, with a focus on how it relates to the concerns of older people as articulated in national and international policy. Chapter Three analyses the general role, structure and processes of the CDBs and whether these can be expected, on their own, to deliver the services and supports needed to address the concerns of older people at local level. Chapter Four looks at the nature and extent of CDB activity in relation to the needs of older people and Chapter Five examines the relationship between the CDBs and older people in terms of perceived effectiveness and consultation. Finally, Chapter Six draws some core conclusions about what needs to be done to improve the attention to older people's concerns in the context of social inclusion processes at local level in Ireland.

Chapter Two

Conceptualising Social Inclusion and Older People

Chapter Two

Conceptualising Social Inclusion and Older People

2.1 Introduction

In order to assess the extent to which the activities of the CDBs are addressing the social inclusion concerns of older people, it is necessary to give some consideration to the concept of social inclusion and how it is applied to older people. This Chapter looks at the overall issues of concern for older people as have been articulated both internationally and in the Irish context. It also examines how the concept of social inclusion has been applied in policy and practice in Europe and in Ireland. Some key features of the broader literature on the concept of social inclusion are also identified, along with an overview of the limited specific attention that has been given to social inclusion and older people in this literature. Finally, conclusions are drawn about social inclusion concept and practice, and how well these relate to the concerns of older people.

2.2 The Policy Context for Ageing

2.2.1 The Madrid International Plan of Action on Ageing

The Madrid International Plan of Action on Ageing (UN, 2002) provides the internationally accepted blueprint for policy on older people. It called for changes in attitudes, policies and practices at all levels in all sectors so that the full potential of ageing in the twenty-first century might be fulfilled. While recognising that the foundation for a healthy and enriching old age is laid early in life, the Plan was intended to be a practical tool to assist policy-makers to focus on the key priorities associated with individual and population ageing. Recommendations for action in the Plan were organised according to three priority directions: older people and development; advancing health and well-being into old age; and ensuring enabling and supportive environments.

The Plan noted that implementation would require sustained action at all levels in order to respond to the demographic changes ahead, and to mobilise the skills and energies of older people. It would also require systematic evaluation to respond to new challenges. It stated that what would be needed would be a political, economic, ethical and spiritual vision for the social development of older persons based on human dignity, human rights, equality, respect, peace, democracy, mutual responsibility and cooperation, and full respect for various religious and ethical values and cultural backgrounds.

This has significant implications for the work of the Irish Government at national and local levels, namely to foster an enabling environment within which central and local government, local development agencies, the voluntary sector and older people themselves can work to effect the necessary changes recommended under the Plan.

2.2.2 The European Approach

In 1999, the UN celebrated the International Year of Older Persons. The European Commission's contribution to the International Year was *Towards a Europe for All Ages: Promoting Prosperity and Intergenerational Solidarity*. It aimed to stimulate policy development within the Member States by outlining the challenges of population ageing and proposing policy responses to these challenges. Four areas of policy relevance were identified:

- employment/labour market
- social protection
- health and care
- equality, anti-discrimination and social inclusion.

The main policy themes are summarised in Table 2.1.

Table 2.1 Policy themes

Theme	Objectives
Adapting employment policies and practices to ageing	■ Higher activity and employment rates at all ages, including later life ■ Equal opportunities between men and women throughout the lifecycle
Adjusting to ageing in retirement and pensions	■ Adapting retirement ages to longer lives and better health ■ Adjusting pension schemes to later and more gradual retirement ■ Providing more equitable and stable pension systems
Responding to needs in health and care through healthy ageing	■ Giving more emphasis to preventative approaches ■ Improving access to health treatment for all ages and for all older persons ■ Providing an adequate supply of quality care for the very old/frail ■ Promoting the role and potential of rehabilitation

More recently, issues relating to older people have been addressed through equality legislation and the development of sustainable models for the provision and funding of long-term care in Europe:

■ Directive 2000/78/EC, *Establishing a General Framework for Equal Treatment in Employment and Occupation* (Council of the European Union, 2000) prohibits any direct or indirect discrimination on the basis of religion or belief, disability, age or sexual orientation

■ EU policy on long-term care is outlined in COM (2004) 304, a communication from the Commission on modernising social protection for the development of high-quality, accessible and sustainable healthcare and long-term care (Commission of the European Communities, 2004). This defines a common framework to support Member States in the reform and development of healthcare and long-term care.

2.2.3 The Irish Policy Context

There is no single comprehensive policy in relation to ageing and older people in Ireland and the Madrid Plan of Action on Ageing has yet to be actively embraced (NCAOP, 2005). However, various elements of a policy agenda for older people have been articulated by the NCAOP, the Equality Authority and the National Economic and Social Forum (NESF).

2.2.3.1 The Equality Authority and the NESF

In 2002 the Equality Authority published a report entitled *Implementing Equality for Older People* (Equality Authority, 2002). This report argued that many of the barriers to older people's participation in society and in the labour market arise from negative stereotyping of older people which influences decision-making. The Equality Authority set out nine principles which underpin their equality strategy for older people:

1. equality with due regard to difference
2. equality with due regard to diversity
3. full legal equality
4. equality of opportunity
5. right and capacity to participate
6. integration of policies and services
7. intergenerational solidarity
8. mainstreaming and age-proofing
9. involvement of all sectors of society.

These principles were then applied to seven key areas of action and recommendations were made for each area.

Following the publication of *Implementing Equality for Older People* (Equality Authority, 2002), the NESF examined the implementation issues arising from the report. The main recommendations made by the NESF were as follows (NESF, 2002):

1. that Government should indicate a likely timeframe in which to implement resource-sensitive recommendations from the Equality Authority report. Recommendations that have little or no cost implications should be implemented as quickly as possible

2. that equality plans and equality reviews should be prepared with the Department of Justice, Equality and Law Reform (DoJELR) and the Equality Authority taking on a monitoring role

3. that there should be investment in mandatory age awareness training across the civil service

4. that a Government agreement should be established on required joint collaboration and a Department should be nominated as lead agency on this issue

5. that the right of older people to age in place should be established as a core value

6. that age-proofing should be introduced and upper age limits removed with regard to data sources and research

7. that age-proofing of policies and programmes should be introduced across Government Departments immediately.

2.2.3.2 NCAOP Submissions to NAPS

In 2001, the NCAOP made a series of submissions to five of the NAPS working groups. In these submissions they clearly set out their policy position on a range of issues outlined below (NCAOP, 2001a, b, c, d, e, f).

In its submissions, the NCAOP emphasised the need to re-focus conceptualisations of poverty beyond that of cash income alone. The Council argued that the additional dimensions of disadvantage highlighted in NAPS, such as unemployment and early education, are of little direct relevance to older people and do little to illuminate the dimensions of life which can lead to severe disadvantage for certain sections of the older population. This issue parallels some of the problems that exist with definitions of social inclusion when applied to older people discussed later in this chapter.

Employment

The NCAOP stated its concern regarding the low numbers of older people in paid employment and argued that during times of economic slump it is seen as legitimate to withdraw them from labour market, while during times of labour shortages policies emerge to encourage older people to remain in or return to work. In this context, the NCAOP recommended that the structural rigidity of the labour market should be eased and that flexible retirement options for older people should be explored.

Housing

The Council's main concern in this regard is to alleviate housing deprivation among those older people who experience poor physical housing conditions and who are unable to remedy defects from their own resources.

Health

In this submission, as well as focusing on general issues relating to health and older people, the NCAOP focused on work undertaken on behalf of two of the most vulnerable groups of older people, those suffering from dementia and those who have experienced or are at risk of elder abuse. The Council set out a series of recommendations in this regard, as follows:

- that the NAPS concept of poverty be refined and elaborated upon so that it relates more effectively to the circumstances of major sub-groups of the population, such as older people

- that the recommendations made by the Council in its report, *A Framework for Quality in Long-Term Residential Care for Older People in Ireland* (NCAOP, 2000) should be implemented. In this regard, it placed specific emphasis on the need to introduce an equitable system of financing long-term care to ensure that the long-term care needs of older people are met

- that the recommendations in the report *An Action Plan for Dementia* (O'Shea and O'Reilly, 1999) be implemented in full

- that community care services be designated as core services and expanded significantly

- that the recommendations in the report *Protecting Our Future: Report of the Working Group on Elder Abuse* (WGEA, 2002) be implemented

- that a comprehensive programme to promote the health and autonomy of older people be provided for in future national strategies.

Rural and Urban Disadvantage

In this regard, the Council argued that rural older people face a greater risk of housing and secondary deprivation, while those aged 75 and over are at greater risk of basic deprivation. In addition, it asserted that recipients of certain pensions (Old Age Non-Contributory Pension, Contributory Widow's Pension and Non-Contributory Widow's Pension) are at particular risk of poverty and at high risk of experiencing deprivation.

Education

One of the key documents that emphasises the contribution of education to the health and well-being of older people in Ireland is *Adding Years to Life and Life to Years: A Health Promotion Strategy for Older People* (Brenner and Shelley, 1998). The NCAOP included the following key recommendations from this report in its submission:

- encouraging and facilitating retired people to be involved in physical, educational, creative and social activities

- encouraging and supporting older people to participate in extra-mural adult education programmes at universities and colleges as part of a lifelong learning process

- enabling older people to become confident users of technology so that they can participate more fully in society

- enabling older people to recognise the growing contribution of technology in promoting independence and improving quality of life (in relation to social stimulation, communication, information, personal development, healthcare, transport, security, surveillance, etc.).

2.3 The Policy Context for Social Inclusion

2.3.1 EU Social Inclusion Policy

Following the recognition under Articles 136 and 137 of the 1997 Amsterdam Treaty that combating social inclusion was one of the fields where the European Union had an active role to play in supporting and complementing the activities of the Member States, the 2000 Lisbon European Council agreed that the Member States should coordinate their policies for combating poverty and social exclusion on the basis of an open method combining common objectives, national action plans and a community action programme.

National action plans for social inclusion (NAPS/inclusion) play a key role in this regard, translating the common objectives into national policies while taking into account national circumstances, national social protection systems and social policies.

The objectives of the first NAPS/inclusion were endorsed by the European Council at Nice in 2000. They were:

■ to facilitate participation in employment and access to resources, rights, goods and services for all

■ to prevent the risks of social exclusion

■ to help the most vulnerable

■ to mobilise all relevant bodies.

The key policy approaches associated with each of these objectives are summarised in Table 2.2.

Table 2.2 Key policy approaches addressing the objectives of NAPS/inclusion

Objective	Key policy approaches

1.1 Facilitating participation in employment	■ Access to stable and quality employment for all women and men who are capable of working:
	  – pathways to employment/training
	  – reconciliation of work and family life, including childcare and dependent care
	  – using the social economy
	■ Improving employability (human resource management, organisation of work and lifelong learning)

1.2 Facilitating access to resources, rights, goods and services for all	■ Social protection systems:
	  – ensure resources to live in dignity
	  – overcome obstacles to employment
	■ Housing and basic services (decent and sanitary)
	■ Healthcare (appropriate to situation, including situations of dependency)
	■ Education
	■ Culture
	■ Justice
	■ Sport and leisure
	■ Transport

Objective	Key policy approaches
2. Preventing the risks of exclusion	■ eInclusion ■ Over-indebtedness ■ Homelessness ■ Family solidarity
3. Helping the most vulnerable	■ Persistent poverty ■ Children ■ Areas marked by exclusion

4. Mobilising all relevant bodies	■ Participation and self-expression of people suffering exclusion
	■ Mainstream the fight against exclusion into overall policy:
	  – national, regional and local levels
	  – coordination
	  – adapting to the needs of those experiencing exclusion
	■ Promote dialogue and partnership:
	  – social partners, NGOs and social service providers
	  – all citizens
	  – businesses

The European approach and an assessment of progress to date was presented in the *Joint Report on Social Inclusion* (Council of the European Union, 2004), and included the following definitions of poverty, social exclusion and social inclusion.

Poverty

People are said to be living in poverty if their incomes and resources are so inadequate as to preclude them from having a standard of living considered acceptable in the society in which they live. Because of their poverty they may experience multiple disadvantage through unemployment, low income, poor housing, inadequate healthcare and barriers to lifelong learning, culture, sport and recreation. They are often excluded and marginalised from participating in activities (economic, social and cultural) that are the norm for other people and their access to fundamental rights may be restricted.

Social Exclusion

Social exclusion is a process whereby certain individuals are pushed to the edge of society and prevented from participating fully by virtue of their poverty, lack of basic competencies and lifelong learning opportunities or as a result of discrimination. This distances them from jobs, income and education, as well as social and community networks and activities. They have little access to power and decision-making bodies, and often feel powerless and unable to take control of the decisions that affect their day-to-day lives.

Social Inclusion

Social inclusion is a process which ensures that those at risk of poverty and social exclusion gain the opportunities and resources necessary to participate fully in economic, social and cultural life, and to enjoy a standard of living and well-being that is considered normal in the society in which they live. It ensures that they have greater participation in decision-making which affects their lives and access to their fundamental rights (as defined in the Charter of Fundamental Rights of the European Union).

It can be seen that the concept of social inclusion as articulated at European level is quite a broad one that, at least in principle, could encompass most of the concerns of older people. However, there are certain factors that act to limit the scope of the concept and how it is applied in practice. One issue is that it is easier to define objective and quantifiable indicators of excluding factors (poverty and unemployment) than positive indicators of participation and influence. For this reason, benchmarking activities within the European NAPS/inclusion process have tended to focus on a fairly narrow range of risk factors for social exclusion.

In addition, some commentators have suggested that the relatively recent emergence of the concept onto European and national policy and practice agendas may not yet have resulted in any significant paradigm shifts of social policy. For example, it has been suggested that there may have been a tendency in some countries to re-package existing policy and practice lines under prescribed social inclusion headings, at least initially (Levitas, 2003). However, the second series of national plans, which commenced in 2003, show a greater development of the concept and this trend can be expected to continue in the third series of plans to commence in 2006.

2.3.2 The Irish Approach

Social inclusion has been on the Irish policy agenda for a number of years and this has been given added impetus by the development of the coordinated approach across EU Member States outlined above. This section outlines some of the main contexts and approaches to social inclusion in Ireland.

2.3.2.1 NAPS and Revised NAPS

The Irish Government agreed a programme of action geared to significantly reducing overall poverty and equality at the UN World Summit for Social Development in 1995. After the summit, a ten-year National Anti-Poverty Strategy (NAPS) was drawn up by an Inter-Departmental Policy Committee and launched in 1997 (Government of Ireland, 1997). A NAPS unit, based in the Department of Social, Community and Family Affairs (DoSCFA), was established to coordinate implementation of the strategy.

Following a review of NAPS, the Government published a revised NAPS entitled *Building an Inclusive Society* in early 2002 (DoSCFA, 2002). This provided a new framework for tackling poverty and social exclusion, and was undertaken in consultation with the social partners as one of the commitments under the Programme for Prosperity and Fairness (PPF). The objectives of Revised NAPS were:

■ to reduce to 2 per cent and ideally eliminate consistent poverty[3]

■ to build an inclusive society and develop social capital within disadvantaged communities.

Building an Inclusive Society also identified vulnerable groups for particular attention including women; children and young people; older people; people with disabilities; and ethnic minorities.

Revised NAPS identified some new institutional structures to underpin the implementation of the Strategy, one of which was the NAPS Social Inclusion Forum. The primary objective of this Forum is to provide organisations and individuals not involved in the social partnership process with the opportunity to contribute to the process of monitoring and developing NAPS (NESF, 2003).

3   Consistent poverty is described by the Combat Poverty Agency as income poverty combined with basic deprivation CCPA, 2004).

No specific definitions of social inclusion or social exclusion were set out in NAPS or Revised NAPS. However, the definition of poverty set out in both strategies was later adopted by NAPS/Inclusion strategies and the CDBs in relation to their social inclusion work:

'People are living in poverty if their income and resources (material, cultural and social) are so inadequate as to preclude them from having a standard of living which is regarded as acceptable by Irish society generally. As a result of inadequate income and resources, people may be excluded and marginalised from participating in activities which are considered the norm for other people in society.'

(Government of Ireland, 1997)

2.3.2.2 NAPS/Inclusion

The first Irish NAPS/Inclusion Plan (2001-2003) was prepared and submitted during the first half of 2001 when a wider, more comprehensive review of NAPS outlined in Section 2.3.2.1 was still underway. This Plan did not contain many specific targets as these were being developed in the context of the NAPS review process and extensive consultation with the social partners.

The current NAPS/Inclusion Plan runs from 2003 to 2005. The core objective of the Plan, as set out in *Sustaining Progress* (Department of the Taoiseach, 2003), is 'to build a fair and inclusive society and ensure that people have the resources and opportunities to live life with dignity and have access to the quality public services that underpin life chances and experiences'. Key related objectives include:

- sustaining economic growth and employment
- providing levels of income support to those relying on social welfare sufficient to sustain dignity and to avoid poverty, while facilitating participation in employment, and to achieve economic independence
- addressing the specific needs of groups at high risk of poverty including tackling the causes of intergenerational transmission of poverty
- supporting disadvantaged communities
- providing high quality public services to all.

In addition, *Sustaining Progress* identified priorities for the 2003-2005 period in a number of special initiatives, which would be the subject of a sustained focus of effort by Government and the social partners.

Although older people are not a specific priority in the current NAPS/Inclusion Plan, Objective 3 does identify older people among the vulnerable groups. In this regard, NAPS/Inclusion emphasises the 'special focus on the needs of the elderly under the various relevant policies in the [Action] Plan. A priority for policy research will be the special needs of growing numbers of older people living alone. Special priority is being given to policy development on the provision of care for the elderly' (Office for Social Inclusion, 2003). In addition, although not directly mentioning older people, many of the objectives include actions that benefit older people indirectly as a function of their implementation. These include income adequacy and security, housing and accommodation, health, provision of care and transport.

Nevertheless, it should be noted that the specific targets for older people set by NAPS/Inclusion restrict their focus to health and heating:

- by 2003, national guidelines will be put in place for the provision of respite care services to carers of older people

- access to orthopaedic services will be improved so that no one is waiting longer than twelve months for a hip replacement

- by 2007, adequate heating systems will be available in all local authority rented dwellings providing for older people.

A review of submissions made to NAPS/Inclusion (Cousins, 2003) reflects this apparent invisibility of older people in national social inclusion policy. In the main, the submissions made on Chapter One of the Plan made no specific reference to older people, even though they were specifically identified as a target group under Objective 3. However, submissions that dealt with policy measures did make specific recommendations on older people's issues including:

- introducing flexible retirement options to allow older people to go on working should they wish to do so

- increasing pensions for older women, including increases in the Qualified Adult Allowance (QAA) to 100 per cent of the Old Age Non-Contributory Pension, and backdating homemakers' disregards

- increasing the stock of lifetime and adaptable housing

- implementing the Equality Authority report on equality for older people (Equality Authority, 2002)

- extending the meals-on-wheels scheme.

One reason for the limited visibility of older people as a target group may be a tendency to over-identify social exclusion with employment. In its position paper on NAPS/Inclusion, the Equality Authority (2001) criticised the national action plans of the EU Member States for their over-emphasis on the role that employability plays in combating social exclusion, and asserted that insufficient attention is paid to the connections between poverty, inequality and social relations, which are complex and often multi-faceted. Without this perspective on the mechanisms of social exclusion, many older people may slip through the net of current national policy.

2.4 Social Inclusion at Local Level

2.4.1 CDBs and SIMs

As outlined in Section 1.2.1, the CDBs were established in 2000 in order to bring about more coordinated delivery of public and local development services at local level. This section looks at the strategy preparation process, the composition of the CDBs, the types of activity in which they engage, the roles of key associated entities including SIMs, and developments that took place in 2004 and 2005.

2.4.1.1 Composition of the CDBs

CDB members (including those from community and voluntary organisations) are nominated as set out in guidelines published in Section Two of *Preparing the Ground for CDBs* (DoEHLG, 1999). The membership of the CDBs is specifically prescriptive across all sectors to ensure that their composition is balanced, and also to avoid Boards becoming large and unwieldy. Members are chosen from four different sectors as listed below:

1. local government – typically seven members (e.g. SPC chairs, Cathaoirleach/ Mayor, county/city managers, urban representatives)

2. local development – two representatives each from County/City Enterprise Boards, LEADER II groups, ADM-supported partnership companies and community groups

3. State agencies – typically ten members as appropriate from the HSE, FÁS, Teagasc, An Garda Síochána, VECs, Department of Education and Science regional offices, county/city childcare committees, Enterprise Ireland, IDA

Ireland, regional tourism organisations, Department of Social and Family Affairs regional officers, SFADCO/Udarás na Gaeltachta

4. social partners – one member each from employer and business organisations, trades unions, agricultural and farming organisations, and two members from community and voluntary organisations.

Overall, approximately 20 per cent of the representation on the CDBs is from the community and voluntary sector. As will be discussed later, however, this does not necessarily mean that the voice of older people is to the fore in this representation.

Along with the establishment of the CDBs, the Interdepartmental Task Force on the Integration of Local Government and Local Development Systems also recommended the setting up of a Community and Voluntary Forum in each county or city. This was a reflection of the Task Force's recognition of the importance of this sector in the social and economic life of local communities, and of their potential for contributing to the cultural development of such communities. The Fora were to be clustered around groups with a focus on social inclusion and groups with a focus on cultural, sporting, recreational and residence-association work. They were to be the medium through which community and voluntary representatives were nominated to the CDBs and other consultative mechanisms, such as Strategic Policy Committees (SPCs) and local authority local area committees. Section Five of *Preparing the Ground for CDBs* (DoEHLG, 1999) deals in greater detail with nomination procedures for community and voluntary representatives.

2.4.1.2 The CDB Strategy Preparation Process

A primary task of each CDB was to prepare and oversee the implementation of a strategy for economic, social and cultural development. The overall aim of the strategy was to provide a shared vision for the development of the area for the following ten-year period. The strategies were to be delivered by the constituent members of the CDBs, each of whom would deliver elements of the strategy through their operational plans and services.

A preparatory period of up to two years was planned, with the strategies to be finalised by January 2002. In order to provide a template for the CDB strategies and ensure that they had a recognisable format and reached a minimum common standard, in May 2000 the Task Force published strategy preparation guidelines in *A Shared Vision for County/City Development Boards* (Interdepartmental Task Force on the Integration of Local Government and Local Development Systems, 2000b). Although the guidelines were designed to be a framework, they were not intended to be a straight-jacket. They consciously avoided being overly prescriptive to allow for local distinctiveness and flexibility in preparing strategic plans. According the these guidelines:

- the CDB strategy should deal with all matters perceived by the Board as important in its county/city, and for that area's future development and welfare, in whatever sector or field

- the CDB's shared vision should be very broadly based and it should go well beyond the traditional boundaries of local development or economic strategies into such key areas as health, education, cultural development, housing, transport and infrastructure

- the CDB strategy should focus on all relevant matters but in particular on specific areas where the CDB felt its existence could 'add value', where it could make some distinct contribution and where something new could be made to happen

- the CDB strategy should focus on areas of possible overlap between bodies, difficulties with coordination, or gaps in service provision

- there should, as emphasised in the NDP, be a very explicit focus on social inclusion.

2.4.1.3 Focus and Types of CDB Activity

In 2003, a review of the CDB strategies was carried out (Fitzpatrick Associates and ERM Ireland Ltd, 2003). This review examined the focus and types of activity of the CDBs, and provides a useful contextual background for the current study.

In terms of the CDBs' overall goals and objectives, the review found that there has been a clear emphasis on quality of life issues, that is, on the provision of the mix of economic, social, cultural and other background factors that citizens require to achieve a high quality of life in terms of work, recreation and leisure, education and training, and housing. Social inclusion actions were found to be the largest single category.

The Task Force guidelines (outlined in Section 2.4.1.2) envisaged that the CDBs would identify and analyse all service providers and levels of service provision in their areas. However, the Fitzpatrick study concluded that most of the published audits are, in effect, directories of service provision rather than analyses explicitly specifying weaknesses or gaps in service delivery. In general, systematic audits of service provision proved difficult, in turn making clear identification of service gaps and/or overlaps difficult.

The review concluded that actions were skewed towards the softer variety of research, planning and networking, rather than rigorously analysing gaps in service delivery. The authors do note, however, that this is perhaps both inevitable and correct as the CDBs are not separate implementing agencies. They are designed primarily to improve working relationships between their existing members with a view to better joined-up delivery of services at local level. As implementation of actions has proceeded, more of these tasks are being carried out by CDBs, mainly proofing, consultation, campaign launching and overseeing pilot initiatives. However, without a budget and with limited authority, many of the other tasks are not achievable by CDBs directly.

2.4.1.4 Structure of the SIMs

The NDP proposed a key role for CDBs in coordinating local delivery of social inclusion measures. To progress this role, a Senior Officials Working Group was set up to 'consider and report on the most appropriate institutional arrangement for coordination and delivery of social inclusion expenditure under the next NDP' (Interdepartmental Task Force on the Integration of Local Government and Local Development Systems, 2000b). This Group reported in April 2000 and recommended a number of specific tasks to be undertaken by central level organisations and by the CDBs at local level.

One proposal concerned the establishment of SIM Working Groups by the CDBs and a circular was issued to this effect. Reporting to the CDBs, the SIMs were established to focus on social inclusion measures included under the NDP and to gradually broaden their scope and reach to include other social inclusion activities in their localities. Their work was to include assessing the extent of coordination existing at local level, ensuring a coherent delivery of measures to target groups and localities, and developing a matrix of local NDP social inclusion measures.

In 2003, the National Development Plan/Community Support Framework (NDP/CSF) Evaluation Unit published an evaluation of social inclusion coordination mechanisms. The purpose of this evaluation was to assess whether the SIMs and CDBs were likely to achieve the objectives of coordination and integration in the delivery of social inclusion measures in the NDP.

The main conclusions of the evaluation were that:

- the strategies largely failed to provide direction in terms of tackling difficult and contentious issues around coordination and integration, such as agency boundaries, overlap and duplication

- the extent of progress and quality of output at the time had been variable

- only minimal progress had been made at national level (in relation to cross-departmental coordination and real support for coordination at the local level)

- the social inclusion coordination process had faced considerable constraints at local level, some being inherent in the organisation of the Irish public administration system. Other constraints identified include the lack of authority underpinning the local coordination function, the absence of incentives for organisations pursuing issues around coordination and seeking to eliminate duplication, the general lack of priority attached to the work of the SIMs, both by Government Departments and local delivery agents, and the non-availability of indicator data for social inclusion measures at county level

- the SIMs had little impact at national level to date on agencies/Departments; at local level they had raised awareness of social inclusion issues among local agencies and stakeholders but there was no clear sense that the SIM process had yet made a difference to service delivery.

A number of recommendations were made in the report including:

'The CDB social inclusion coordination process should shift from one of a focus on the coordination of organisations and delivery structures to a focus on outcomes for socially excluded groups.'

The Evaluation Unit recommended that this shift in focus should be implemented as follows:

- each CDB should identify a limited number of target groups (maximum of three) for immediate attention, each of which should be a tightly defined subset of the NAPS categories

- each CDB should prepare an integrated target group plan in respect of each of the identified target groups within one year

- these plans should include an analysis of the current situation of the target group, details of current social inclusion provisions by agency for the target group, a set of quantified objectives, agreement on the responsibilities and role of each organisation involved, and realistic performance indicators.

Clearly, it would be of great benefit for the progression of social inclusion measures for older people at local level if the SIMs could be encouraged to identify older people as one of the priority target groups to be addressed in this manner.

More generally, however, one of the main conclusions that can be drawn from all of this is that the envisaged role of the SIMs has been subject to change over time and that they have not had the opportunity to develop into a cohesive vehicle for ensuring systematic and coordinated attention at local level, either to social inclusion issues in general or to the specific concerns of older people in particular.

2.4.2 The Local Development Social Inclusion Programme (LDSIP)

A central objective of the NDP was to tackle social exclusion and at the same time achieve sustainable economic and employment growth to consolidate the country's competitiveness and foster economic development. One measure of the social inclusion and childcare priority of the NDP is the LDSIP set up in late 2000.

The LDSIP addresses the needs of the 15 target groups identified in the NDP, one of which is older people. It is structured into three target action areas known as sub-measures: services to the unemployed; community development; and community-based youth initiatives. Any activities relating to older people are grouped under the community development sub-measure of the LDSIP.

Work with older people is being developed and implemented by most of the LDSIP partnership companies and community partnerships. Examples of this work include activities associated with setting up new groups led by older people, including active age groups, facilitated by development workers. For example, County Leitrim Partnership has initiated work of this nature, with the support of the North-Western Health Board's Physical Activity Programme (PALS).

2.5 Conceptualisations of Social Inclusion and Older People

2.5.1 Some Core Themes in Social Inclusion Discourse

The conceptualisation and definition of social inclusion can vary considerably within policy, practice and research. Sometimes there is quite a degree of specificity in the concept, for example in the emphasis in the European approach on the most marginalised groups in society. This poses the question of whether the focus should only be on marginalised older people, such as older people at risk of poverty, or whether social inclusion addresses a broader range of older people's concerns. On the other hand, the term social inclusion is often used quite loosely, with many or

58

all 'social' issues being put into the social inclusion basket. This raises the question of whether or not the concept brings any special added value over and above more defined sociological perspectives, such as those focusing on equality, addressing poverty, active citizenship, neighbourhood renewal and so on. In this case, the concern is that the particular social issues that arise for older people may be less clearly identified and targeted because of the looseness of the concept.

However, despite the ostensibly broad coverage of the European approach, in practice the focus of social inclusion policy and discourse can often be quite narrow, concentrating on what Levitas (1998) terms a 'social integrationist' discourse that emphasises paid work as the primary or sole legitimate means of integrating individuals of working age into society. This is very different to the 'redistributive' discourse that was dominant in the field of social policy in the 1980s and 1990s, which understood social exclusion as a complex concept with a focus on dynamic, multi-dimensional and relational aspects. The social integrationist discourse focuses on active labour market policies and its negative implications for social welfare payments. Although this perspective is now beginning to include attention to labour market participation of people beyond the normal working age range, there is the risk of losing sight of the main concerns of the majority of older people, which are typically engaged in aspects of their lives other than employment. In addition, resources and interventions may concentrate on the needs of the labour market rather than society as a whole, including older people.

More generally, aside from the European focus on poverty and access to employment, the interpretation of the scope of social inclusion can vary widely. For example, many people would consider it to include attention to issues such as:

- equal opportunities
- discrimination
- rights
- recognition
- participation in decision-making
- social participation
- human capacity-building
- social capital-building.

All of these elements are important for the status, participation and quality of life of older people.

An approach to social inclusion that caters for the full range of concerns of older people needs to address:

- at-risk older people
- issues that apply across the older population because they relate to the particular life stage that they represent (recognition, status, equality/anti-discrimination, socially valued roles etc.)
- specific themes that are important for many older people (health and social services, active retirement, social participation etc.

2.5.2 Conceptualising Social Inclusion as It Relates to Older People

Overall, relatively little focused attention has been given to exploring how the concept of social inclusion relates specifically to the concerns of older people. One exception is the review of research in this field by Phillipson and Scharf (2004). In this study, the research reviewed suggested that some groups of older people may be more at risk of social exclusion than others, for example:

- those affected by *cumulative (life course) disadvantage and persistent poverty*, e.g. women without occupational pensions, homeless older people, and older people from some ethnic minority groups
- those affected by *contracting social networks*, e.g. older people experiencing loneliness and intense social isolation, older people without informal carers and single person households
- those affected by *area disadvantage*, e.g. older people residing in inner city communities subject to economic and social decline, and older people living in remote rural communities characterised by a loss of services and amenities
- those marginalised through *physical and mental ill-health*, e.g. the frail elderly with multiple chronic conditions
- those affected by the operation of *ageist beliefs and practices*, e.g. older people seeking employment or access to particular services
- those *cut off from new technologies*, e.g. older people without access to the Internet
- those who experience *difficulty in exercising their civic rights*, e.g. older people not registered to vote, and older people who find contact with legal and advice services problematic.

The review found that four key factors have been indicated in these processes: age-related characteristics; cumulative disadvantage; community characteristics; and age-based discrimination.

Age-related characteristics refer to the way in which older people are disproportionately affected by certain kinds of losses or restrictions relating to income, health or reduced social ties. Such changes can take place right across the life course but they are likely to feature more prominently in later life given retirement-associated income changes, the impact of chronic disabling conditions and increased needs among people adjusting to living alone.

Cumulative disadvantage refers to the fact that birth cohorts may become more unequal over time. For example, limited educational and work opportunities at early points in the life course may in the long-term lead to reduced income in older age or limited awareness about how to access the full range of health and social services.

Community characteristics refer to how older people, who may have strong attachments to their locality, may also be vulnerable to changes associated with population turnover, economic decline, and rising levels of crime and insecurity in neighbourhoods.

Age-based discrimination refers to the impact of ageism on economic and social policies that contribute to various forms of social exclusion in old age. This aspect has been the focus of recent work by the NCAOP and by the Equality Authority.

Against this background, and building on a review of different approaches to measuring social exclusion, Scharf and Smith (2004) suggest that older people may experience, in one or more of the following forms, exclusion from:

- material resources

- social relations

- civic activities

- basic services

- neighbourhood networks.

From this perspective, it could be concluded that the definition of social exclusion employed in Partnership 2000 and in the NDP might cater better for the broad range of concerns of older people than definitions that focus primarily on income and employment:

■ 'marginalisation from production' could encompass issues relating to employment, unemployment, retirement and lifelong learning among older people, including those in the older segment of the traditional 'working age' population and those who are older than this

■ 'marginalisation from consumption' could include not just issues of poverty but also modes of participation, such as involvement in the Information Society, eCommerce etc.

■ 'marginalisation from networks' could include issues of social participation and involvement, loneliness, carers and caring etc.

■ 'marginalisation from decision-making' could include the extent to which the voices of older people are heard in decision-making and how older people's interests are represented in decision-making structures and processes

■ 'marginalisation from an adequate quality of life' could include a range of important areas for older people, such as transport, housing, and health and community services.

Apart from this, there are some other aspects that must be considered in developing a suitable concept of social inclusion to address the spectrum of issues of importance for older people.

One set of challenges is posed in relation to how labour market engagement relates to social inclusion for older people. In this context, exclusion discourse and policy that focuses on work and employment leaves the position of older people who have permanently withdrawn from their occupational roles unclear. For example, in their production domain of exclusion, Burchardt *et al.* (1999) judge as 'included' and 'engaged in a socially valued activity' those who have reached State retirement age and are retired. This contrasts with research in social gerontology that highlights the exclusionary impact of retirement on many older people (Phillipson, 1998).

62

Another set of challenges arises from the emphasis in exclusion debates on the dynamic nature of social exclusion (Byrne, 1999). There are now a variety of panel studies available that show how people move in and out of poverty/exclusion as their circumstances change (Leisering and Walker, 1998; Burchardt, 2000). The evidence from such studies leads to the conclusion that, as Perri 6 (1996) asserts, 'most people get out of poverty' and that the boundaries of exclusion are essentially fluid rather than rigid. In the case of older people, however, it may be that, for those prone to exclusion, the experience of being excluded may be maintained on a longer-term basis than for other groups, e.g. older people who lack adequate material resources are unlikely to be able to get out of poverty without financial support from the State.

Finally, challenges are also posed in relation to the neighbourhood dimension of exclusion, and its impact on older people's sense of identity (Scharf et al., 2002). For many reasons, the local residential environment may represent a much more important aspect of inclusion for older people than for other age groups. Firstly, older people tend to spend more time than younger people in their immediate neighbourhoods. Secondly, many older people have spent much of their lives in a particular neighbourhood, deriving a strong sense of emotional investment both in their home and surrounding community (Phillipson et al., 2000).

2.6 Conclusions

Despite an extensive amount of policy work on social exclusion at Irish and European levels, and much parallel work on the social and other concerns of older people, there is still a tendency for older people in particular to remain largely invisible in discourses about social inclusion and exclusion. It has been argued that the focus on labour market participation as an indicator of social exclusion can itself act to exclude older people from adequate consideration within this domain. More generally, the current operational definitions of social inclusion must be expanded to give a fuller scope to the concept if it is to reflect the range of older people's concerns adequately. If this is not done, there is a strong possibility that social inclusion policy-making at local level will not take into account the needs of older people that are unrelated to labour market considerations, and that older people will be prevented from effectively communicating their needs to local agencies and from participating meaningfully in important decisions in their community.

64

Chapter Three

How the CDBs Work

Chapter Three
How the CDBs Work

3.1 Introduction

This chapter examines the role, structures and *modus operandi* of the CDBs and associated entities, and also whether these, as currently operating, can be expected to deliver on the social inclusion needs of older people at local level. Data is drawn from documentary analysis and interviews carried out with representatives of the CDBs. Qualitative analysis consisting of coding emerging themes in the interviews was carried out. This means that codes may not occur in all interviews, or may occur more than once in a single interview. Because of this, percentages are not used in presenting findings as they would be misleading and confusing.

3.2 Priority Setting: CDB Approaches and Processes

Interviews with representatives of the CDBs indicated that three main approaches were utilised by CDBs when setting priorities: consultation; research; and establishment of working groups. Most CDBs employed more than one of these approaches. Three interviewees, however, stated that they had not engaged in prioritisation of social inclusion areas. One CDB had attempted to use the nine grounds of the Equal Status Act, 2000 as a framework for its strategy and treated each of these equally.

Table 3.1 How social inclusion priorities are set by CDBs

Approach	Number of CDBs
Consultation	20
Research	12
Working groups/themes[4]	8
Other	11

4   Those CDBs that identified cross-cutting themes were unlikely to identify particular target groups as well,
     which would explain why older people were not identified as a target group for specific consultation.

In addition to these three approaches, representatives of 11 CDBs also stated that the CDB played an important role in setting priorities. In some cases, findings from research or consultation were brought directly to the CDB, which had responsibility for identifying appropriate measures or actions. In others, the SIM identified themes or target groups and forwarded these to the CDB for ratification, though incidences of this were less frequent.

3.2.1 Consultation

The extent and nature of consultation varied across CDBs. However, it was clearly the principal method used in determining priority areas for social inclusion measures, with 20 interviewees stating extensive consultation was undertaken when compiling the CDB strategy. Some focused primarily on statutory agencies and local government players, and some included broader consultation with community and voluntary interests. Older people's organisations were directly consulted by some CDBs and this aspect is discussed in greater detail in Chapter Five. A smaller number held public consultation processes, including public meetings, seeking submissions on published strategy documents, and through local media and schools.

3.2.2 Research

The most frequent type of research undertaken was auditing existing social inclusion measures and spend, as well as existing services, with the objective of identifying gaps and aspects needing attention. Templates developed in the context of the NDP were typically used to guide this type of research. Poverty profiling aimed at identifying priority groups was also reported by a number of CDBs, typically using NAPS indicators. Other approaches included SWOT analyses, compilation and analysis of baseline data, and targeted research on particular sectoral themes (e.g. crime, education and health), or surveys of community and voluntary organisations. Some research included specific attention to older people and this is discussed in greater detail in Chapter Five.

3.2.3 Working Groups/Themes

Another common approach was to identify key themes for attention and for working groups to be set up to develop these. Sometimes the themes were initially identified through consultation and/or research, and then taken up by specific working groups. The tendency was towards identification of thematic areas rather than specified target groups.

3.2.4 Other Approaches

Finally, 11 CDBs employed a range of additional methods for determining priority areas. Three CDBs used templates from NAPS or the NDP to prioritise marginalised groups. Two CDBs prioritised existing RAPID work programme areas, while a further two CDBs set priorities through discussion within local authority structures (namely the CDB in one case and the Social Inclusion Task Force in the other). One CDB handed responsibility for the development of its strategy to a third-level institution. In another CDB area, a pre-existing local authority strategy formed the basis for prioritising areas for the CDB strategy. A further CDB used the results of the NDP/CSF evaluation to assist in prioritisation at a later stage, while another asked local development agencies to prioritise areas for social inclusion work.

3.3 SIMs

3.3.1 Activity Levels of the SIMs

Results from the current research found that the activity levels of SIMs and the frequency of SIM meetings vary considerably across the country, although nearly all of the SIMs were described by interviewees as being 'active' or 'very active'. Definitions of what 'active' meant varied across interviews. In some cases, activity was described solely in terms of frequency and regularity of meetings, and in others in terms of activities undertaken and outcomes of meetings held.

Frequency of meetings ranged from monthly or bimonthly to biannually. In some CDB areas, the national requirement on SIMs to undertake endorsement and cohesion activities has led to more frequent meetings than originally planned. In addition, representatives of four CDBs stated that the SIM in their area had taken over responsibility for the RAPID programme.

Interviewees from three CDB areas did not feel that their SIMs were very active. This was put down to lack of commitment and a high turnover of representatives in one instance, the impact of national requirements regarding cohesion and endorsement in another, and poor decision-making skills in the third.

Finally, one interviewee stated that the role of the SIM in their Board area was not to oversee implementation of the strategy (this being the responsibility of the social and health review group) but to focus on specific social inclusion work programme areas.

3.3.2 Definitions of Social Inclusion

Representatives of the CDBs and SIMs were asked to provide a working definition of social inclusion as espoused by their SIM or CDB. Of those interviewed, 28 discussed this issue. A high degree of variation was found across the SIMs regarding their definitions of social inclusion.

Seven interviewees said that their CDB used the definition of poverty from NAPS:

> 'Our definition of social inclusion comes from the National Anti-Poverty definition.'

> 'We've been keeping to the NAPS really ... we keep that as our standard.'

Interestingly, one interviewee, while stating that the NAPS definition of poverty was the underlying definition, went on to say that in practice the SIM and CDB tried to avoid using formal definitions of poverty and social exclusion as they had found in the past that these could alienate people and prevent them from participating effectively:

> 'We try to steer away from definitions ... because it's scaring people ... you see people stiffening up so we adapt our own, whatever suits somebody, conscious of the Government one, trying to make it tangible.'

Another CDB had done something similar, using the NAPS definition for the work of the Board as a whole, but using a broader definition in the CDB strategy:

> 'In our strategy we would have included social inclusion – quite a broad definition looking at the whole concept of community development, empowering people to engage as citizens in all the processes ... '

Two interviewees said that the SIM in their areas used the definition of social inclusion set out in Partnership 2000:

> 'We looked at the Partnership 2000 definition of social inclusion from the very start ... and that really was the basis for the strategy and all the way through really.'

'The SIM would have adopted the one that's in Partnership 2000.'

Still other SIM groups (n=4) adapted existing Government definitions to suit their own particular situation, either using sources such as the Equal Status Act, 2000, or adapting NAPS and Partnership 2000:

'We're trying to follow the nine grounds as per the Equal Status Act.'

One interviewee expressed a concern that existing definitions of social inclusion were not suited to rural contexts:

' ... the particular target groups in a rural situation that would be socially excluded mightn't necessarily be socially excluded in an urban situation ... they mightn't readily be identified as socially excluded [under NAPS].'

Three interviewees said that their CDBs came up with their own definitions of social inclusion, independent of Government or academic sources. Two interviewees said that their CDBs based their definitions on previous work carried out by the SIM. The third did not give further information on how their definition was developed.

Of those interviewed, 12 interviewees did not provide a clear definition of social inclusion. However, there are a number of factors which should be taken into account in this regard. One interviewee clearly stated that there was no definition of social inclusion in the CDB strategy and did not provide a definition at the time of interview. However, on examination of the strategy, a definition of social exclusion was provided: 'social exclusion [is] essentially those processes, structures and influences that work to exclude people from the "good things in life"'. Another interviewee did not quote the definition but referred the interviewer to the CDB strategy. On examination of the strategy, it was found that the CDB had adopted the Partnership 2000 definition. Three interviewees argued that social inclusion as a concept was very difficult to define, and questioned the ability of a single formal definition to cover the needs of very different target groups:

'Is it totally necessary that everybody has a common understanding when my work is in education and my understanding of social inclusion is based on the target groups that I work with?'

Two interviewees were SIM board members rather than CEDOs. Both of these gave definitions used by the then health boards, as they both worked in this sector.

3.3.3 Barriers to SIM Activity

During the course of the interviews, some specific factors were identified by the interviewees that pose barriers to SIM activity.

3.3.3.1 Lack of Support at National Level

This was an important factor identified by nine interviewees. It was felt that there was a lack of clarity at national level about the ultimate direction and role of the CDBs and SIMs. In addition, there was a perception that the coordination and integration tasks of the CDBs and SIMs were not paralleled by a similar undertaking at national level. This was particularly the case with regard to the task of tracking NDP social inclusion spend:

> 'I firmly believe that national Government and the two or three Departments involved aren't clear about the final picture, and that's causing immense confusion on the ground on behalf of everybody,'

> 'I think that all of the CDBs are being undermined by a lack of support at national level for the work of the agencies that are trying to do things a little bit differently at the local level, and we're being asked to do something at the local level where there is no corresponding determination at the national level of coordination and cohesion.'

> 'Specifically I'd be referring to our role in terms of tracking NDP social inclusion spend in the county, I mean that's been a nightmare piece of work with no real help or guidance or assistance at national level.'

3.3.3.2 Requirements to Endorse Local Development Plans and Engage in Integrated Target Group Planning

Eight interviewees saw this as a key factor. They felt that the requirements of national Government had placed a heavy burden on SIM members in the absence of adequate resources. This had the effect of diverting SIMs from other tasks (i.e. overseeing and tracking implementation of social inclusion measures):

> 'More and more, the SIM's agenda is driven from a national level. So what you would find is something called the Joint Ministerial Initiative led by the Department of Community, Rural and Gaeltacht Affairs (DoCRGA), come with proposals around an integrated target group plan and that becomes the work

of the SIM to do. So just as a time and resource issue, they spend most of their time trying to implement what comes from a national level.'

'An awful lot of things were coming down the line to [the] SIMs. They were having to deal with things in a very tight timescale, for example the endorsement with very little guidelines ... that sort of carry on [...] meant that SIMs were always fire-fighting ... '

3.3.3.3 Lack of Resources

Seven interviewees identified lack of resources (budgetary, staff and administration) as a barrier to SIM activity. One interviewee identified the lack of staff and administrative structure as placing a significant restriction on the implementation of decisions made by the SIM. Another interviewee powerfully illustrated the lack of resources in this regard:

'It doesn't have its own administrative structure, or ... its own complementary staff [to] assist with the implementation of the work of SIM, which I think is a shortfall.'

'We don't even have the money to buy tea and coffee when they meet, we have no resources and I really have to stress that.'

3.3.3.4 Other Barriers

Other barriers cited included:

- difficulties with project tracking software (n=6)
- tension between SIM representatives from different organisational backgrounds (statutory, local authority, NGO and voluntary/community sector) (n=5)
- failure to meet regularly and poor follow-up to actions agreed at meetings (n=3)
- time pressures on SIM members (n=3)
- failure to understand the role of the SIMs and how agencies could bring their work down to focus at a local level (n=2)
- lack of authority of SIMs at local level (n=2).

Since the establishment of the CDBs and SIMs, and the publication of the CDB strategies, a number of developments have taken place at the instigation of the DoEHLG and the DoCRGA.

3.4.1 Mid-Term Review of CDB Strategies

In January 2005, each CDB was asked to carry out a review of its ten-year strategy. It was intended that the review should focus on the CDB's core coordination role and result in:

- the selection of a limited number of key priorities and actions on which the CDB would concentrate over the following three years

- a focus on integrative actions aimed at a more joined-up approach to local service delivery involving relevant agencies.

It is not envisaged that the findings of the review will result in fundamental changes to the overall strategies. For example, it is likely that the strategic vision and SWOT analysis of the city or county identified in the strategy will remain in place. However, it is likely that some adjustments, refinement and rebalancing in priorities and implementation arrangements will be required in the light both of developments and of experience to date. The review is due for completion by December 2005.

3.4.2 Review of Community and Voluntary Fora

A review of the Community and Voluntary Fora was carried out by a working group of Directors of Community and Enterprise, and the DoEHLG in 2004. The review was conducted in consultation with the community and voluntary sector at national level, as well as representatives of each Forum at a series of regional meetings. A questionnaire was also sent to Directors of Community and Enterprise in each local authority area in relation to the experience of the Fora to date in their areas. Arising from the review, a series of recommendations was made which each Forum was requested to implement.

3.4.2.1 Structure

- Where it has not already happened, Fora should develop local area fora and/or sectoral/thematic networks in order to maximise participation and interest. In particular, Fora should have an identifiable and active cluster around social inclusion.

- All Fora should have a means of actively involving groups with a social inclusion focus, in particular for representational purposes as set out in the guidelines *Preparing the Ground for CDBs* (DoEHLG, 1999).

- It is also important to ensure that as wide range of groups as possible is on the Forum, so that it is inclusive and representative.

- Community and Enterprise sections in local authorities should prepare (where not already done) or update a register of community and voluntary organisations in their county/city.

3.4.2.2 Operation

- All Fora should have an agreed constitution/statement of operating principles (it should be noted that this is now a requirement of Community and Voluntary Fora funding allocations).

- While encouraging Fora to engage support for their operation from a range of possible sources, it is important that the role of CEDOs as the main contact points for Fora within local authorities should continue.

- Fora should continue to meet regularly and an annual meeting schedule should be set out in advance.

- More regular meetings of network/clusters and area fora should be developed in addition to the county/city level meetings.

- All Fora should continue to prepare annual work plans and should review their implementation on Fora need to support and develop the active participation of member groups.

3.4.2.3 Relationship with CDB

- All community and voluntary representatives to CDBs, CDB-related structures and Area Committees, as expanded, (where relevant) should be drawn from the Community and Voluntary Fora.

- The recommended clustering arrangements should continue whereby CDB representatives are selected from the social inclusion and general clusters respectively.

- Community and Voluntary Fora should be closely involved in the implementation of CDB strategies, as appropriate. A useful mechanism is to ensure that the Community and Voluntary Fora are represented, from the appropriate clusters, on relevant CDB implementation/working groups, where this is not already the case.

3.4.2.4 Relationship with County/City Council

- It is recommended that for future community/voluntary representation on SPCs, the Community and Voluntary Fora would be invited by the county/city council to nominate their representatives.

3.4.2.5 Support

- As a general principle, the capacity of the Community and Voluntary Fora should be encouraged to grow in order to facilitate them to take responsibility for their own organisations' operations. While the support of the Community and Enterprise Office (in particular CEDOs) is extremely important (as well as, in some cases, support from local development agencies), such support should always be provided in the context of building the capacity of the Fora themselves. Community and Enterprise Offices (Directors, CEDOs, clerical/administration staff) should continue to prioritise support for Community and Voluntary Fora in their own work plans.

- Other CDB member agencies (in addition to local authorities and local development agencies) should be encouraged to provide support and resources for Fora in their area.

3.4.2.6 Development

- It is important that the Fora continue to be developed with particular reference to their involvement, as appropriate, in the operational plans of CDBs and their member agencies. In addition, the following means of further developing the Fora should be pursued:
  - training and capacity-building
  - greater focus on work plans
  - continued development of relationships with statutory and local development agencies
  - development of issue-based/sectoral/thematic networks.

3.4.3 The Joint Ministerial Initiative on the Review of Local and Community Development Structures and Programmes

This ongoing initiative involves the DoEHLG, the DoCRGA and the DoJELR. Its aim is to allow greater scope for cooperation and coordination in the delivery of local services. As part of this initiative, in February 2004 the Government approved a range of measures to improve local and community development services on the ground, including:

■ requesting community and local and community development groups across urban, rural and Gaeltacht areas to propose improvements in their respective areas by mid-2004. This was done in order to avoid overlap, duplication and confusion and was overseen by the CDBs

■ earmarking funding to support specific proposals for improved cohesion across local and community development bodies which emerged from the above process. The funding was to be spread over three years (2004-2006) and targeted at providing better services. It was to be administered by the DoCRGA. In 2004, funding allocations to CDBs under this initiative totalled €2,904,300

■ asking CDBs to consider and endorse work plans prepared by community and local development agencies

■ advising that except in exceptional circumstances, Departments or public bodies wishing to set up new schemes within the sector should do so within existing structures instead of setting up new layers in an attempt to ensure that more money would earmarked for services instead of administration.

3.5 Conclusions

The CDBs and SIMs were established primarily to fulfil a coordination and integration role at local level. In this context, the success of the measures identified in their strategies will depend on the follow-through by the agencies within whose scope of implementation responsibility for the various measures reside.

Overall, the interviews indicated that CDBs use a variety of different definitions of social inclusion. Most of them derive their definitions from either NAPS or Partnership 2000, or a combination of the two. Interestingly, questions were raised as to the applicability of formal definitions of social inclusion to development work at local level, and some CDBs adapted the concept of social inclusion to their own particular context. The possibility also exists that different agencies at local level are using different definitions of social inclusion. The implications of this for the coordination role given to the SIMs could not be explored in the current study and warrants further investigation.

In addition, the research identified a number of factors that appear to have been inhibiting the extent of involvement of older people, and the visibility and attention to issues of concern to older people at CDB level. Recent developments aimed at improving the Community and Voluntary Fora processes offer the potential to improve some aspects of this situation. Furthermore, the review of the CDB strategies taking during 2005, as well as the ongoing Joint Ministerial Initiative on the Review of Local and Community Development Structures and Programmes, offers an opportunity to encourage greater attention to the concerns of older people and reinforce the involvement of older people in CDB-related processes, if mechanisms can be put in place in a timely manner to give this the necessary impetus.

78

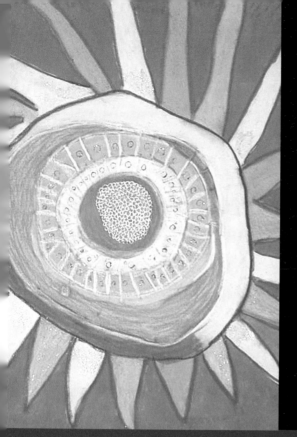

Chapter Four

The CDBs and the Promotion of Social Inclusion of Older People

Chapter Four

The CDBs and the Promotion of Social Inclusion of Older People

4.1 Introduction

This chapter presents an analysis of what the CDBs are doing, or planning to do, to promote the social inclusion of older people at local level. The scope and focus of the analysis is first outlined. Three main types of action of relevance for older people at CDB level are then introduced – direct delivery of services for older people via CDB member agencies, coordination of services for older people, and support for involvement of older people in the CDBs and other processes of importance for them. The remainder of the chapter focuses on the range of specific initiatives that fall within the first two categories. The final category, focusing on the involvement of older people, is addressed separately in Chapter Five.

4.1.1 Scope and Focus of the Analysis

The CDB strategies provided the principal information source for the analysis of the measures being planned or undertaken that address the concerns of older people. They were judged to be the most appropriate source from which to develop a comprehensive overview, given that the strategies are intended to provide a detailed statement of what the CDBs plan to engage in during the 2002-2012 period.

It was impossible to obtain objective and standardised information across the CDBs regarding implementation of relevant actions in the strategies. Data from the interviews indicated a high level of uncertainty regarding which measures had been implemented and what stage they were at. This can in part be explained by difficulties in the installation of project-tracking software. It was originally envisaged that a single IT-based online tracking system would be used across all CDBs to monitor implementation of the strategies. However, significant delays were encountered in the development of this software. In the interim, many CDBs chose to pursue alternatives; either purchasing commercial packages, using pre-installed database facilities or using paper-based monitoring. This has led to delays in setting up formal and reliable monitoring of implementation, and has meant that information is highly variable and difficult to compare across CDBs.

4.1.2 Structure of the CDB Strategies

Each of the 34 CDB strategy documents is structured slightly differently and the language to describe the various levels in the overall structure also differs. In general, however, each strategy begins with a vision for the county or city, which is then typically broken down according to a number of main themes. Goals are established for each theme, with each goal supported by a number of key objectives that are necessary to achieve the goal. Each objective is underpinned by key strategic actions that are necessary to achieve the objective. Responsibility for achieving an action is allocated to a nominated coordinating mechanism or lead partner/agency. These agencies or partners are required to develop a work plan based on the strategic actions and issues identified within the strategies.

The analysis of the documents was prepared in two stages. First, a profile of each CDB's planned and ongoing measures in relation to older people was prepared[5]. These profiles were then analysed and synthesised in order to provide an overview of what is being done at CDB level across the country, as well as to identify relevant patterns and themes, and is presented in the sections that follow. Percentages are used as data was derived from quantitative analysis of the contents of the strategies. (In addition to the analysis presented in this chapter, a number of interesting examples of social inclusion activities were described in the interviews with representatives of the CDBs and representatives of older people. These are included in Appendix Two.)

The focus of the analysis in this chapter is on the actions that the CDBs have specified as being directed towards the concerns of older people. In addition, many of the CDBs promote actions with a more general focus that can also be of benefit to older people, even if they are not directly identified as a specific target group. Examples of such general actions would include primary and community care initiatives, and actions relating to crime, safety and security. Because the central interest was to examine the manner and extent to which older people's

5   The profiles are available online at http://www.ncaop.ie/research_list.html.

needs appear on the agendas of the CDBs, the analysis only includes those actions where older people were specified as the main target group and those actions with a wider and more general scope where older people were specifically identified by the CDBs as one of the target groups expected to benefit.

4.1.3 Types of Approach

The analysis of the CDB strategies identified three quite different approaches to addressing the concerns of older people:

- direct actions to be carried out by member agencies
- coordination related actions
- actions focusing on involving older people in policy and planning.

Direct actions to be carried out by member agencies are tangible measures to deliver specific benefits to older people through CDB member agencies. *Coordination related actions* include the establishment of structures and mechanisms to improve inter-agency and inter-organisational cooperation, development of integrated strategies, planning activities and so on. *Actions focusing on involving older people in policy and planning* are those with the objective of giving older people a voice in CDB processes and in the community generally. Figure 4.1 indicates the percentages of CDBs that have addressed the concerns of older people in their strategies in these various ways. A number of the CDBs addressed the concerns of older people through two or sometimes all three of these types of action.

Figure 4.1 Types of approach addressing the concerns of older people identified in CDB strategies

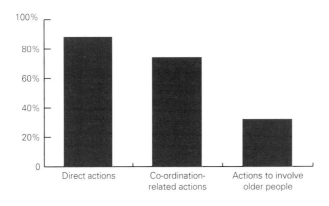

Direct actions were the most frequently found measure, being included in the strategies of the majority of CDBs (88 per cent). A wide range of social inclusion themes and specific types of action were found. Table 4.1 shows the distribution of these themes across the strategies of the 34 CDBs.

Table 4.1 Social inclusion themes being addressed by direct actions in CDB strategies

Theme	CDBs addressing theme
Housing	71%
Health and community services	68%
Safety and security	50%
Education and lifelong learning	41%
Social and recreational	35%
Transport	32%
Access to public services	24%
Intergenerational and community development	21%
Work and retirement	21%
Accessible public places	12%
Gender-related	12%
Income	3%

4.2.1 Housing

Housing was the most frequent theme for direct actions relating to older people, being addressed in 24 (71 per cent) of the CDB strategies. Many of the safety and security measures also have a housing dimension as do some independent living initiatives classified under the health and community services theme, so the total number addressing housing can be considered higher.

Table 4.2 lists some of the main ways that housing issues for older people are being addressed in the strategies. Three themes occur most frequently:

■ making more sheltered housing available

■ design of housing to meet needs posed by ageing and disability

■ supports for home maintenance and improvement.

A broad mix of approaches was identified, including public sector provision, awareness-raising and incentives for the private sector, and usage of the social economy. In some areas that have seen extensive population growth the issue of including older people in new housing developments is also on the agenda.

Table 4.2 Housing

General	■ General actions to meet the housing needs of older people; provide a variety of housing services at a reasonable cost and appropriate to the needs of older people
Sheltered housing/ independent living	■ Provide appropriate sheltered housing/supported living/independent living arrangements for older people so that they can live independently ■ Develop flexible housing settlements for older people allowing them to remain in their community within an adaptable and supported environment ■ Examine the potential of developing a pilot community development independent living facility ■ Promote a multi-agency and community-based approach to planning housing for older people and people with a disability, taking into account the accommodation needs of carers and personal assistants
Design for ageing/ disability	■ Promote Design of Housing schemes for older people that are disability-friendly; encourage accessible and suitable housing stock through development of 'lifelong homes', adapted housing, awareness-raising, support services, incentives etc. ■ Provide suitable accommodation for deaf/hard of hearing adults with mental health/behavioural problems, medium-term assessment centre for deaf people with additional problems and a high support unit for older deaf people ■ Provide retirement homes for older adults with disabilities

Home maintenance and improvement	■ Put in place the necessary supports and resources for older people to upgrade their homes
	■ Upgrade local authority accommodation facilities of older people and people with disabilities and identify the requirements for upgrading of existing local authority accommodation
	■ Develop a coordinated scheme to improve the quality, insulation, energy efficiency and accessibility of non-local-authority housing stock, particularly that occupied by older people
	■ Provide repairs to housing for older people through social economy projects
	■ Publicise the Essential Repairs Grant and the Special Housing Aid for Older People so as to increase the uptake of these grants
Including older people in new housing developments	■ Begin pilot actions on housing provision for older adults and people with disabilities in new estates, to include lifetime adaptable homes
	■ Ensure that a percentage of new housing is set aside to provide for people with disabilities and the older population
Housing for older people in isolated areas	■ Develop a special strategy to provide appropriate accommodation for older people living in isolated areas

4.2.2 Health and Community Services

Health and community services was the next most frequent theme for direct actions relating to older people, being addressed in 23 (68 per cent) of the CDB strategies. Some of the safety and security measures (in particular those relating to prevention of accidents in the home and to social alarm services) also have a health and community service dimension as do some independent living initiatives classified under the housing theme, so the total number addressing health and community services can be considered higher.

Many of the actions are pitched at a fairly generic or systemic level addressing issues such as:

- implementation of existing plans via their member agencies
- development of integrated community care plans
- increased levels of service provision
- research to identify needs and project demand
- development of the full range of services from home to residential care.

This is not unexpected, given the coordination function of the CDBs and the fact that the main responsibility for the health theme lies with the Health Service Executive (HSE) Areas. A lot of attention was also given to supporting carers of older people and to developing partnership approaches with the community and voluntary sector. All of the main levels of service – home help and other home care, community and day care centres, and residential services – received a good deal of attention.

Overall the main thrust of the proposed measures is towards improving basic home, community and residential services, reflecting the poorly developed state of current core health and social care services for older people. An interesting trend is the development of facilities for older people in island communities (e.g. Sherkin Island and Inis Mór).

Table 4.3 Health and community services

General/ systemic	■ Implement, via member agencies, existing strategies and plans for health and care services for older people
	■ Develop integrated community care plans focusing on the healthcare needs of older people
	■ Establish county inter-agency forum on services for older people; facilitate the creation of strategic alliances between all agencies and organisations providing services for older people in order to bring about the development of cohesive packages of care
	■ Increase the provision of key services as part of the community care plan with specific focus on the needs of older people – public health nursing, GP services, home help services, paramedical, social work services, day care services
	■ Improve the quality and increase the availability of hospital, day hospital and residential care for older people and provide it as near as possible to their own homes or communities
	■ Conduct research on/audit existing service provision for older people in order to identify need for the provision of necessary facilities; assess the current demand levels and projected future demand, develop a county plan for care of older people
	■ Develop targeted and community-based initiatives for older people and people with disabilities, so that they can choose to live in their own homes with appropriate personal care and other supports
	■ Provide a range of interventions in the home, in community and acute hospitals, and in care centres for older people; develop facilities to meet the needs of the older person, e.g. step-down facilities, day hospital and day centre; develop Community Care Units for older people
	■ Ensure that appropriate are services are available; carry out an audit of existing nursing home facilities and home help care within the county
	■ Maximise the potential cross-border cooperation in relation to the provision of hospital and emergency services and community services, i.e., cross-border links and exchanges relative to health and social gain of older people and people with disabilities

Carers	■ Provide a range of support to carers; extend the availability of home services and respite care services throughout the county; work in partnership to expand support and services for carers in the home; explore new ways of providing health and social care to older people and to support carers/families in their responsibilities of caring ■ Resource and develop the support services for carers adequately; establish and resource a support group for carers; increase the number of respite facilities and short-term respite services including day care and night sitting, particularly at the weekends ■ Provide eldercare services to enable carers to participate in other activities ■ Provide quality and accessible information on a range of issues for carers ■ Conduct research in order to establish the level of relief services needed by carers ■ Provide new and alternative care services to replace the decrease in care traditionally provided by family members
Partnerships with community groups	■ Continue to support community groups in the provision of support services, such as shopping, visiting and transport ■ Support community and voluntary organisations in providing core services (care for older people, childcare, etc.) when possible thus implementing the principle of subsidiarity ■ Develop networks for older people ■ Provide support for local branches of the Alzheimer Society to apply for a social economy project for their home support service
Access to services	■ Improve the access of older people to mainstream health and social care facilities ■ Target older people as a group 'at risk' of not accessing services and develop a coordinated response
Home help	■ Extend the hours allocated to older people through the home help service with additional hours allocated at evenings and weekends ■ Re-examine the criteria for applying for the home help service, as the means test often prevents people from applying

	■ Review the role and duties of the home help services; investigate the feasibility of carrying out domestic duties or essential duties, such as transport to the doctor or shopping
	■ Provide home helps for older people on discharge from hospitals to cover convalescence period
Day care	■ Assess needs for day care; implement action plan on the basis of identified needs
	■ Expand the number of day care centres for older people, and integrate day care services with other community services throughout the county
	■ Provide additional day care units with transport services, paramedical and shower facilities
Residential care	■ Develop affordable and appropriate residential care options
	■ Lobby for the review of the regulations concerning nursing homes in order to take account of the social and psychological needs of older people
	■ Provide an activities nurse, or trained staff, to stimulate the long-term residents
	■ Provide physiotherapy services in long-stay wards
Healthy lifestyles	■ Research the issue, identify good practice and implement programmes to encourage physical activity among older people
	■ Develop an integrated programme to promote healthy living by building upon existing strategies with respect to older people care and other (specified) areas
	■ Promote smoking cessation programmes targeting older people
	■ Provide training courses on nutrition for older people for health professionals working in the community
	■ Provide nutrition training for voluntary groups preparing community meals, home helps and carers
	■ Provide 'being well' courses for older people's groups in the community
	■ Provide seminar on ageing activity with particular emphasis on attitude and health promotion

Involvement of older people	■ Facilitate the participation of older people in conjunction with voluntary and statutory social care providers in reviewing existing services with a view to developing suitable and effective social care provision
Elder abuse	■ Research the issue and identify good practice; implement programme to combat elder abuse ■ Develop programmes to highlight and make people aware of the signs and symptoms of elder abuse
Respite	■ Provide a dedicated unit for residential and respite care for patients with Alzheimer's Disease ■ Support the provision of occupational therapy and physiotherapy services during client's stay in respite
Social alarms	■ Provide alarms to vulnerable older people and those discharged from hospital
Aids and appliances	■ Implement new streamlining procedures and structures for access to aids and appliances
Paramedical services	■ Provide a mobile chiropody service and employ additional opticians, occupational therapist and physiotherapist to reduce the present waiting list
GPs	■ Review the system of evening and weekend cover by GPs
Dementia/ Alzheimer's Disease	■ Undertake specific actions in relation to older people suffering from Alzheimer's Disease or other forms of dementia – increased home support, day care, respite and residential services ■ Increase the number of long-term and respite beds for individuals with Alzheimer's Disease ■ Increase the number of day care facilities for older people with dementia; provide a day care unit for individuals with Alzheimer's Disease in addition to the current general day care unit
Stroke	■ Develop multi-disciplinary stroke care teams to operate from hospitals and other regional and local healthcare facilities

A number of CDBs also proposed measures relating to healthy ageing including initiatives addressing themes such as nutrition and smoking. In addition, in the interviews with CDB representatives there was a tendency for physical activity and sports-related initiatives for older people (e.g. the Go For Life and PALs programmes) to be categorised as health-oriented measures. These are addressed later in more detail under the social and recreational theme.

Apart from those initiatives focusing on physical activity, the strategies had fewer measures oriented directly towards older people themselves. For example, empowering older people to better manage health issues received little attention. Nevertheless, the interviews did identify a number of innovative approaches in this area.

4.2.3 Safety and Security

Measures to address safety and security issues for older people were also strongly represented, with half of the CDBs including such measures in their strategies.

Table 4.4 Safety and security

Security in the home	■ Arrange for Community Gardaí to visit older people's groups to discuss safety and security issues
	■ Increase cooperation between An Garda Síochána, the Western Health Board (WHB), agencies and voluntary groups at community level to improve security in the home for older people
	■ Improve security in the home through the expansion of the Special Housing Aid for Older People programme throughout the county
	■ Promote measures to enable older people to protect themselves against property crimes (including fraud) and violence
	■ Install increased security devices in housing programmes for older people
Safety in the home	■ Encourage falls prevention training and initiatives targeting older people in the community
	■ Encourage fire prevention training initiatives targeting older people in the community
	■ Support the provision of smoke detection and security systems in all rural dwellings occupied by older people

	■ Increase awareness of public safety issues particularly those affecting women, older people, young people, racial and other minorities
	■ Promote knowledge and use of safety features for preventing accidents in the home, especially targeting children under 5 years and older people
ICT	■ Lobby for the use of modern technology to provide more security particularly for the most vulnerable members of society, i.e., security systems for older people and scheme of community support for older people
	■ Promote an enhanced partnership/multi-agency approach incorporating ICT to crime prevention
Personal/social alarms	■ Develop a uniform county-wide system for the use of personal alarms by older people
	■ Provide training to voluntary and community groups that provide security devices to older people to make them aware of the needs and concerns of older people
	■ Subsidise the monitoring charge for alarm systems
	■ Lobby for change in current policy regarding alarms for older people
Community initiatives	■ Promote the Meitheal concept by supporting initiatives such as 'Reach Out – Be a Better Neighbour' with a specific focus on older citizens of the county, in order to ensure that the national average mortality rate among older people in winter (currently the highest in Europe) is reduced through greater community awareness and monitoring
	■ Involve communities in preventing crime in their local areas by becoming actively involved in Neighbourhood Watch and Community Alert; encourage the establishment of active Neighbourhood Watch schemes and their expansion, particularly in rural areas with high concentrations of older people living alone
	■ Develop and implement schemes around safety in the community, ensuring consultation with older people as equal participants

Both security against crime and safety from accidents in the home featured strongly in the strategies. Community measures such as Neighbourhood Watch schemes and development of personal/social alarm services were most common.

4.2.4 Education and Lifelong Learning

Access to education for older people, especially those aged over 65, is an important issue. The research found that measures to address this theme were quite strongly represented, being found in 14 (41 per cent) of the CDB strategies.

Table 4.5 Education and lifelong learning

General	■ Encourage older people to participate in education and training courses ■ Create programmes for older people to address education needs including ICT; develop targeted training programmes to allow older people to enjoy a fulfilling life ■ Develop lifelong learning opportunities for all ages within the Gaeltacht
Community-based	■ Encourage outreach information and training to all in rural areas, specifically target older people for inclusion in community classes ■ Develop and pilot a number of taster training programmes in community facilities throughout the county for older people ■ Develop community-based skill interventions for key groups such as older people ■ Investigate the potential for a pilot initiative between the library and older people to promote the library as a valuable resource in the community
Involvement of older people	■ Utilise the experience of senior citizens as a resource in the development of education/training programmes (mentoring) ■ Implement a Training of Trainers programme to develop the capacity of older people to train other older people in ICT skills ■ Develop the potential of older people and retired employers/employees in relation to ICT training and assess usage by working with the Forum for the Elderly and other groups

ICT	■ Develop ICT training for older people
	■ Make ICT networks and facilities available throughout the county
	■ Deliver and evaluate the CAIT programme with a view to extending it throughout the county
Third-level	■ Explore the possibility of establishing a degree course specifically for older people to meet new emerging needs in today's society
	■ Establish third-level facilities in the Gaeltacht, so students of all ages can have third-level access
Information	■ Ensure that the information needs of older people are adequately and innovatively addressed; information sessions in communities on rights of older people, on health information and to publicise local clubs and activities
	■ Provide home helps and carers with information on the rights and entitlements of older people
Work-related	■ Provide training for people aged 55+ to work in the tourism industry
Specific groups	■ Develop a new senior Traveller education and resource centre

With regard to education and training, some CDBs identified older people as a target group at a general level. Others were more specific, with a number of themes occurring in more than one strategy. Addressing older people in community-based training was one such theme. Involvement of older people in the design and delivery of training was also a feature of a number of strategies, while ICT training also featured in a number of strategies. Other themes addressed included participation in third-level education, information, work-related training and the educational needs of older Travellers.

Interviews with CEDOs, members of SIMs and older people's representatives revealed a strong focus on ICT training for older people. Eight CEDOs and members of SIMs described ICT training initiatives either planned or ongoing for older people in their areas. This is in the context of the national focus on developing such technologies, and consequent fears of the risks of a 'digital divide' growing between those who can access ICT and those who cannot. Older people are clearly at risk in this regard. However, many counties in which IT training programmes had been implemented found uptake and retention of older students quite difficult. It was perceived that older people were often wary of new technology and encountered difficulties in learning how to use it.

4.2.5 Social and Recreational

Measures addressing the social and recreational theme also featured quite strongly, with 12 (35 per cent) of the CDBs including these in their strategies. Apart from general initiatives, sports, physical activity and the Arts featured. Some CDBs also focused on the involvement of older people in the running of social and recreational activities of relevance for older people.

As regards sports and physical activity, the Go for Life and PALs programmes were mentioned a number of times in the strategies and also in the interviews. Age and Opportunity work in partnership with health boards, each of which has a Go For Life Co-ordinator and Local Sports Partnerships. PALs has been rolled out across the country and there appears to be a high level of awareness about the programme among older people and community workers alike.

Table 4.6 Social and recreational

General	■ Develop a range of programmes to meet the social and recreational needs of older people in partnership with local communities
	■ Work with existing older people's organisations/bodies to increase participation by older people in sport, recreation and leisure, and promote awareness about the benefits of participation in exercise
	■ Encourage and increase the participation of older people in various community activities through day care centres and active age groups
	■ Provide older people with meaningful activities based on their needs; encourage groups to affiliate with Age and Opportunity or the Federation of Active Retirement Associations (FARA)
Physical activity	■ Establish a partnership approach to the development of physical activity for the older adult involving the Local Sport Partnership, statutory agencies, clubs, leisure centres, active age groups etc.
	■ Work closely with active age groups to encourage them to include regular physical activity on their agenda; develop and support the Age and Opportunity Go For Life programme

	■ Develop and implement an integrated promotional campaign to communicate the benefits of regular physical activity for the older adult highlighting opportunities for participation
	■ Support groups in their applications for grant aid towards the purchase of equipment for physical activity
Sport	■ Broaden non-competitive participation by increasing the range of sport and leisure activities available to target groups such as early school leavers, Travellers, older people etc.; target 'non-traditional' sports groups such as women, older people, social groups and people with a disability, and encourage usage of swimming and leisure facilities
	■ Carry out Age and Opportunity's physical activity project Go For Life in local clubs in collaboration with the Irish Sports Council
	■ Encourage sports clubs and leisure centres to include an older adult representative on their committees; provide improved access for the older adult to participate in sports and recreational activity
	■ Organise events such as a sports festival aimed at introducing older adults to a range of recreational sports
The Arts	■ Develop a programme of creative/community arts activity with older people; pilot a programme using art forms to promote the creativity and self-esteem of older people
	■ Bring theatre into local schools, local residential areas for those who wouldn't normally be able to access theatre throughout the programme of access arts, e.g. young offenders, older people, people with impaired mobility
	■ Pilot an intergenerational Arts programme undertaken in both institutional and non- institutional settings to measure the positive impact on both older and young people
	■ Carry out a study on art therapy for older people and marginalised groups
Reducing isolation	■ Put sufficient measures and actions in place to prevent older people living in isolation
	■ Coordinate people visiting older people in their homes, thereby increasing social contact and alleviating loneliness
	■ Develop clubs in local suitable venues with transport provided
	■ Develop programmes that target older men at risk in rural communities; pilot an older men's group to address the issue of male isolation

Information and awareness	■ Provide information on the activities available for older people ■ Host an annual exhibition event of projects and services for older people in the county
Involvement of older people	■ Establish a forum to advance a sports and recreation strategy focusing on the needs of various target groups e.g. older people and marginalised groups and the development of formal input structures, thereby enabling people of all ages to participate in the creation and management of community facilities
Meeting places	■ Make a room available in libraries that will act as a meeting place for older people
Specific themes	■ Actively seek to provide new areas of minority activity and pilot three local programmes engaging youth, middle-aged and older people in the areas of dance, hill-walking, computers, photography and music/sound

4.2.6 Transport

Transport for older people was another theme that occurred quite frequently in the strategies, with eleven (32%) of the CDBs including this in their strategies.

Table 4.7 Transport

Rural transport	■ Address the needs of older people in the context of the rural transport audit; provide transport for senior citizens so that they can access public services and link with Rural Transport Initiative ■ Provide grants to support transport provision in areas where there is lack of services ■ Provide support for the work of the Rural Lift in the provision of rural transport services ■ Support the extension of public transport services in rural areas through mini-buses
Accessibility	■ Develop an accessible transport programme for older people ■ Ensure the maximum number of vehicles for licensed public hire are accessible to older people and people with disabilities ■ Introduce an awareness programme for service providers to enable them to cater for the needs of people with reduced mobility

	■ Encourage Bus Éireann to consider those who have mobility difficulties when replacing the existing fleet
	■ Provide appropriate passenger waiting facilities
Public transport	■ Ensure that public transport infrastructure and services meets the needs of older people
Private services	■ Lobby for the extension of free bus passes to all private transport ventures including hackney vehicles
	■ Support the extension of the Free Taxi scheme to cover all modes of transport
Urban transport	■ Make community buses available to older people to enable them to participate in social activities
Specific groups	■ Provide supervised transport to and from day care units for older people with dementia and Alzheimer's Disease

Rural transport issues and accessibility of transport for older people were most frequently addressed in the strategies. Other themes addressed included improved public transport in both urban and rural areas, access to private transport services and the needs of specific groups.

4.2.7 Access to Public Services

The theme of access to public services was addressed by eight (24 per cent) of the CDBs. Equality of access, information and appropriate customer service were the aspects most frequently included.

Table 4.8 Access to public services

Equality	■ Develop good practice guidelines on the prevention of age discrimination for mainstream service providers, promote these guidelines to service providers for implementation within their organisations
	■ Ensure equality of access for all to public services including older people and people with disabilities; identify requirements of people with disabilities and older people to ensure equal access to public services
Information	■ Improve availability of information on entitlements to older people; develop an older person's information pack; update and produce a county-specific older people's information pack and facilitate presentations and discussions of information contained in the pack

Customer service	■ Ensure information and application forms are available through a wide range of outlets and ensure information officers are available to give presentations whenever required
	■ Provide assistance in the completion of forms when requested
	■ Provide awareness training on the needs of older people to relevant people working in public agencies
Consultation	■ Consult older people in the design of services aimed at them
Rural areas	■ Develop a programme to improve access to services for older people in rural areas
Web accessibility	■ Make websites accessible to people with disabilities and older adults, and offer website developers in the county assistance to incorporate national and international guidelines in their work

4.2.8 Intergenerational and Community Development

The theme of intergenerational and community was addressed by seven (21 per cent) of the CDBs. A number of these measures focused on intergenerational activities, especially on encouraging interaction between younger and older people. Two strategies addressed broader community development themes, with measures to include older people in these.

Table 4.9 Intergenerational and community development

Intergenerational	■ Create opportunities where younger and older people can meet and mingle in their own community, by organising intergenerational activities at community level; develop and pilot integrated training programmes for older and younger people to reduce age barriers within the community
	■ Promote mutual understanding between older and younger people through joint activities and examples of good practice
	■ Lobby the Department of Education and Science (DoES) to include visiting older people in their homes as part of Transition Year curriculum
	■ Encourage greater interaction between youth and older people in the county to the mutual benefit of both groups; develop a project with youth and older people's groups which would involve a sharing of skills and talents

| Community development | ■ Devise a programme of events/activities to build community spirit and encourage family and community interaction, particularly among long-established and new residents, including devising programmes for older people including 'reminiscence finders' to be included in a county museum |
| | ■ Ensure neighbourhood civic pride to involve and welcome everyone particularly groups and communities of interest that need to be reached out to e.g. older people, ethnic minorities, children, people with disabilities etc. |

4.2.9 Work and Retirement

The theme of work and retirement was also addressed by seven (21 per cent) of the CDBs. Most measures focused on provision of preparation for retirement courses. Some also gave attention to opportunities for voluntary working in the community. Very few addressed paid employment for older people.

Table 4.10 Work and retirement

Preparation for retirement	■ Improve the availability of retirement planning courses in the county and specifically engage employers to plan such courses as part of HR allocation of staff development time; outline opportunities for voluntary activity/part time work for retired people
	■ Provide older farmers on non-viable farms with the support to leave farming with dignity; provide comprehensive information in relation to the Farm Retirement scheme
Active retirement	■ Encourage the development of active retirement clubs throughout the county utilising existing community resource centres/family resource centres etc.
	■ Provide information to older people and those approaching retirement on the opportunities for volunteering or returning to work or education
Voluntary work	■ Facilitate the contribution of older adults to the community and voluntary sector; establish a volunteer resource centre in the county

Older workers	■ Promote awareness of ageism within the workplace; develop and deliver an awareness programme
	■ Provide training for people aged 55+ to work in the tourism industry
People with disabilities	■ Develop a five-year plan to look at the area of retirement services for older people with disabilities

4.2.10 Accessible Public Places

Four (12 per cent) of the CDB strategies addressed the theme of accessible public places for older people. Apart from generally improving accessibility, specific themes included providing benches in shops and public places, provision of public conveniences and improving parking facilities.

Table 4.11 Accessible public places

General	■ Eliminate access barriers for all through good road layout and design practices for roads, footpaths etc., especially for older people, people with a disability and young families. In the long-term create accessible environments in all developments including access to amenities, businesses and shops, restaurants and provision of accessible toilet facilities
Specific	■ Place more benches at critical and safe locations throughout the county to create an environment where older people especially can be more active
	■ Work with businesses to place seats in shops reserved for older people and people with disabilities
	■ Publish a plan to improve and increase pedestrian crossings in the county
	■ Make public conveniences available on a 24-hour basis at key locations throughout the city, suitable for use by people with disabilities, older people and children
	■ Cater adequately for older people, people with disabilities and people with children in the plans for convenient off-street parking in towns throughout the county

4.2.11 Gender-Specific Issues

Four (12 per cent) of the CDB strategies addressed gender-specific issues. For men, the needs of single men living alone and long-term unemployed men were included. For women, access to ICT training and specific health needs were addressed.

Table 4.12 Gender-specific issues

Men	■ Research the issues specifically affecting men, and in particular older men living alone; develop and implement a plan of action based on needs identified ■ Ensure that in terms of service delivery, specific emphasis is placed on the needs of marginalised men, including long-term unemployed older men and the accommodation needs of single and separated men
Women	■ Continue to develop and implement innovative projects for disadvantaged women and women over 50 years old in line with the NDP ■ Provide additional supports to encourage younger mothers, older women, rural women and women in poverty so that they can participate in ICT training ■ Recognise that women have distinctive health needs and require special consideration in the health service; support the provision of funding to specific groups working with older women, refugee/asylum seekers and women with disabilities to carry out research on their health needs

4.2.12 Income

Only one CDB strategy directly addressed income issues for older people, in the context of actions to address groups at risk of poverty. In this regard, one of the interviewed CEDOs felt that preconceptions held by agencies of the needs and concerns of older people, particularly that the only income concerns affecting older people are to do with pensions and supplementary welfare, prevented the development of local actions centred on improving income levels for older people:

> 'Income, that has been a very difficult one for us to crack here. It has been difficult for agencies to get their heads around it, because they say "Well, the Government has said how much the pension will be or the supplementary welfare allowance". People don't really see what else they can do.'

The focus in this section is on coordination-related activities at CDB level; activities in specific thematic areas (such as healthcare) have been identified, where they occur, in the previous section. As might be expected given the coordination role of the CDBs, coordination-related measures were very common, being found in the strategies of the majority (74 per cent) of CDBs.

There was considerable diversity in the types of action identified, including planning, putting older people on the agenda, vision formulation, service integration, inter-agency coordination, needs identification, development of structures and awareness-raising. In general, there seems to be greater emphasis on softer measures in this area, such as raising awareness and putting older people on the agenda rather than on harder measures to analyse and redress any gaps in service delivery for older people that are arising because of coordination problems. In general, the impression is of a tendency to follow existing agency structures and boundaries in addressing the various themes, with little evidence of a real move towards service coordination (e.g. between transport and health or education services).

Table 4.13 Coordination-related actions

Planning	■ Develop and put forward a long-term plan for the future development of activities and services for older people, taking into account the increasing older population
	■ Coordinate suitable and targeted resources, supports and services to enhance the well-being of older people in the city
	■ Set up a strategic plan to meet the needs of older people in the county catchment area
Putting older people on the agenda	■ Seek to ensure that those at risk of exclusion (including older people) are not left out when planning initiatives, including in the ICT sector
	■ Incorporate the older age profile of the county into planning development and incorporate services for older people in the new County Development Plan

Service integration	■ Establish an integrated service that links current services providing support for establishing and running childcare, afterschools and oldercare services through the stages of business start-up, facilities, planning and legal requirements, and the training and provision of qualified personnel
Inter-agency coordination	■ Develop mechanisms for effective cross-agency coordination of services for older people to ensure that older people get the best possible range of services given available resources ■ Strengthen linkages and information exchange between statutory agencies and voluntary organisations involved in the provision of accommodation, health, education, access and services to older people, Travellers, ethnic minorities and ex-prisoners ■ Coordinate the work of all relevant agencies in relation to programmes for older people
Needs identification	■ Identify and meet the needs of older people
Development of structures	■ Support the development of a Working with Older People Forum in the county whereby all agencies and groups working with older people can meet and update each other regularly ■ Develop a social inclusion unit among agencies of the CDB to promote social inclusion policies among staff in addition to developing pilot projects with groups such as older people
Awareness-raising	■ Increase the awareness of services available to benefit older people among agency staff meeting older people in the course of their work and continue to encourage visits to older people as part of the work of people such as the Gardaí, community wardens etc.

4.4 Actions Focusing on Involving Older People in Policy and Planning

As indicated in Table 4.1, fewer than one third of the CDBs included specific actions to facilitate the involvement of older people either in CDB-related planning, *ab initio*, or in other ongoing development activities in the area. Among those indicating such activity, quite a variety of specific activities were identified, including:

- involvement in the CDB

- needs identification/consultation

- development work

- establishment of new structures

- development of existing structures

- networking of older person's organisations.

Table 4.14 indicates the types of objectives and actions that were identified under each of these themes across the relevant CDBs.

Table 4.14 Actions focusing on involving older people in policy and planning

Involvement in the CDB	■ Facilitate the inclusion of older people in the Community Forum
	■ Put in place mechanisms to ensure that older people are consulted with regard to their own particular needs; request the Community and Voluntary Forum to examine ways of achieving this objective and make recommendations to the Board
Needs identification/ consultation	■ Establish, support and maintain an older people's network to identify the needs of older people and develop appropriate responses to these needs
	■ Create and operationalise links between older people, agencies and community-based groups/projects, ensuring consultation with older people as equal participants
	■ Consult older people in the design of services aimed at them

	■ Facilitate the participation of older people in conjunction with voluntary and statutory social care providers in reviewing existing services with a view to developing suitable and effective social care provision
Development work	■ Seek funding to employ a development worker to develop appropriate responses to work with older people
	■ Develop appropriate methods of involving marginalised older people in programmes, especially those aged 65+ living alone in both urban and rural areas
Establishment of new structures	■ Establish an older people's advisory committee at county level to develop improved coordination between both statutory and voluntary providers, with representation from statutory providers, voluntary sector providers and older people's organisations
Development of existing structures	■ Develop and strengthen fora for older people
	■ Further develop the network of older people's groups in the county
Establish networking of older person's organisations	■ Establish a network of older people's organisations/ voluntary groups; facilitate networking of active retirement groups
	■ Develop networks for older people

As implementation of all social inclusion actions (via lead agencies) has been slow and varies across CDB areas, it is not possible to draw conclusions about the extent of involvement of older people based on the above information alone. Therefore, both CDB and older persons' organisation interviewees were asked to give their own assessments and views on this aspect. Findings from both are set out in Sections 5.1 and 5.2.

4.5 Older People in the Integrated Target Group Plans

In 2004, the DoEHLG published *Improving Local and Community Development Structures and Programmes* (DoEHLG, 2004). This responded to the recommendations of both the mid-term review of the NDP (NDP/CSF Evaluation Unit, 1999) and the NDP/CSF evaluation of social inclusion coordination mechanisms (NDP/CSF Evaluation Unit, 2003) and requested that each CDB prepare an integrated target group action plan for one priority target group identified under NAPS. At the time of interview, four CDBs had selected older people as their target group, or had included older people in the remit of their target group. Table 4.1 lists these CDBs and the target groups in their proposed plans. Although the development of integrated target group plans was seen as placing an extra burden on SIMs, many CDB representatives also saw the plans as providing an opportunity for translating the coordination role of CDBs and SIMs into concrete action on the ground.

Table 4.15 Overview of integrated target group plans targeting older people

CDB	Target group	Comments
Donegal	Older people aged 65+ years	Older people were chosen as a result of a poverty profile of the county. Older people emerged as a significant group. The initial target group was to be older people living along and older women living alone, however the CDB recommended that all older people aged 65+ years be covered.
Leitrim	Farming women, marginalised women aged 65+ years, asylum-seekers and Traveller women	Leitrim is conducting separate plans for each of these target groups.
Monaghan	Older people	Consultation was carried out with older people and their advocates. This indicated a lack of awareness and understanding of their needs. The SIM therefore prioritised older people for the integrated target group plan.
Roscommon	Isolated older people in north-west Roscommon and marginalised men throughout the county	A consultation process carried out for the community development projects in the county highlighted the needs of isolated older people.

Overall it can be concluded that the CDB strategies include a significant amount of planned activity addressing the concerns of older people. As expected, coordination-related activities featured strongly. Considerable diversity was found in the aspects of coordination being addressed in the strategies. There was not much evidence of a concerted effort to assess thoroughly the extent to which there are existing gaps in services for older people that arise from a lack of inter-agency coordination nor of concrete initiatives to provide truly joined-up services for older people at local level. In addition to the expected coordination activities of the CDBs, a large number of proposed direct actions to address the concerns of older people were also found in their strategies. In general there was a tendency towards actions in the fields of housing, health and community services, and safety and security, reflecting the perhaps more obvious basic needs for services and supports that can arise as people grow older. There was also some evidence from some of the strategies and interviews of a move towards recognising older people's need for independence and participation in decisions that affect their lives, such as independent living initiatives and participatory primary healthcare projects.

While education and lifelong learning featured quite strongly in the strategies, the extent to which these have been or will be taken up by older people remains to be seen. It is important that the financial, legislative, emotional and social barriers that prevent older people from accessing educational opportunities are recognised and specifically addressed if these initiatives are to have successful outcomes.

The success of the PALs and rural transport schemes could be seen as good practice models for future initiatives in their respective areas, as both received almost uniform praise from representatives of SIMs, the community and voluntary sector, and older people.

There was a general lack of focus on themes including work and retirement, accessible public spaces, gender-specific issues and income. In particular, the current debates about older people and the labour market do not yet seem to have been addressed to any significant degree in local level actions. This may be related to some of the issues discussed in Chapter Two of this report, particularly the negative stereotypes of older people which shape decision-making (Equality Authority, 2002) and the employment of income-focused definitions of social inclusion and exclusion in European and national policy (Council of the European Union, 2004; Government of Ireland, 1997).

Overall, there was considerable diversity across the CDBs in the themes of relevance for older people being addressed in the strategies and, within a given theme, in the specific issues being addressed. While this may, in part, reflect differences in local needs and priorities, it also suggests that there is not yet a common understanding among the CDBs of the full range of concerns of older people and how these can be addressed at local level.

110

Chapter Five

CDBs and Older People: Effectiveness and Consultation

111

Chapter Five

CDBs and Older People: Effectiveness and Consultation

5.1 Introduction

This chapter examines the nature and extent of involvement of older people in the CDBs. The principal information sources were interviews with CDB representatives, older people and older people's representative organisations in CDB areas. In addition, some information on actions aimed at supporting the involvement of older people was extracted from CDB strategy documents.

5.2 Interviews with CDB Representatives

All 34 interviewees were asked to describe how much input older people and the organisations that represent them have in the process of identifying social inclusion actions for older people in the county strategies. They were also asked whether older people were identified as a distinct group with regard to consultation.

5.2.1 Levels and Types of Input

Table 5.1 provides an overview of the levels and types of input from older people and their representative organisations. Representatives of 14 CDBs reported that they had held targeted consultation with older people or representative organisations. Seven said that while older people were not consulted as a distinct group, they had been represented in general public consultations. The remainder of those interviewed did not report any direct mechanisms for input by older people or their organisations.

Table 5.1 Levels and types of input

Approach	Number of CDBs
Targeted consultation with older people/older people's organisations as a distinct group	14
Older people/older people's organisations included in general public consultations	7
No direct mechanism for input by older people/older people's organisations	13
Total	34

5.2.1.1 Targeted Consultation with Older People/Older People's Organisations

A range of different methods were used to consult with older people directly. The most common method employed was to utilise existing older people's groups (active retirement or senior citizens' groups) or voluntary/local development organisations to contact older people (n=7). For example, one interviewee described an interesting approach, which combined both local agencies and older people themselves:

'... after the SIM group had identified older people as a target group to be worked with, the different development agencies that were around the table were asked to bring representatives of their organisation who would be older people to the next meeting, so there was a meeting then with the development agencies and older people.'

Another approach cited by two interviewees was to set up a consultative forum dedicated to older people. In one case this forum covered more than one CDB:

'We met the older people and we went through the list of things ... stuff like accommodation, health, transport, rather than the other way round.'

Two CDBs held one-off events, such as a focus group with older people or a day-long event:

'We organised, in conjunction with Age and Opportunity, a Forum 55+ in [county] ... we had workshops and so on, and we brought speakers together. There were a couple of hundred people there on the day.'

Other methods used included a specific consultation process and regular ongoing consultation with older people:

> 'We tried very hard to involve and consult with older people. Three groups were consulted ... and older people themselves were included.'

5.2.1.2 Older People/Older People's Organisations Included in General Public Consultation

Interviewees from seven CDBs stated that older people were represented through general consultation mechanisms, mainly the Community and Voluntary Fora. One interviewee stated that while older people were not specifically targeted for consultation about the health section of the CDB strategy, they did constitute part of a wider group formed for this purpose:

> 'I remember when we were consulting for the health section of the strategy we brought the [health board] to do a facilitated workshop for a wide range of people and we did have older people there.'

Another interviewee cited the local ARA as an important group that was well-represented in public consultations:

> 'The Active Retirement Group were cropping up everywhere because they were organised and delivering a fair amount services already across the country. So they were fairly well represented.'

5.2.1.3 No Direct Mechanism for Input by Older People/Older People's Organisations

Interviewees from 13 CDBs offered no evidence of having consulted with older people. Although it may be that older people are represented via Community and Voluntary Fora in some of these cases, this was not expressly identified in the interviews.

5.2.2 Perceived Difficulties in Consulting Older People

A number of interviewees expressed some concerns about the feasibility of consulting older people. These could be grouped into three main themes:

- ■ lack of organisation of older people's representative groups
- ■ difficulties in accessing isolated older people
- ■ general attitudes to older people.

5.2.2.1 Lack of Organisation of Older People's Representative Groups

One factor identified by interviewees that was felt to mitigate against the involvement of older people in the work of the CDB was a perceived lack of organisation in representative groups for older people. Nine interviewees reported this to be a problem. The following quote illustrates how this is seen to affect the SIM's ability to engage effectively with older people:

> 'We don't have a coordinated older people's group in [county]. For that reason it is harder to work with them because they probably come under health rather than under the SIM type things because they are not a single group you can approach to do actions. As a target group they are difficult to engage with because we don't have a body that we can engage with.'

It was felt that organisational difficulties prevented representative organisations from operating at a sufficiently strategic level to allow them to engage fully with the CDB or SIM:

> 'A lot of older groups are social groups rather than campaigning groups. They did not appear to be hugely interested in the consultation process. There is no real umbrella organisation for older people and this has made the task of accessing older people a problem.'

One possible way to improve consultation with older people suggested by an interviewee was to make sure that issues to be discussed were presented in concrete and specific terms in order to reduce confusion and the risk of misunderstanding between both parties:

> 'A better model of consultation is that you have something very specific that you put on the table for feedback … and say "what do you think about this, give us some feedback."'

5.2.2.2 Difficulties in Accessing Isolated Older People

Four interviewees were worried about the tendency to rely on ARAs and the difficulties involved in accessing more vulnerable or isolated people not involved in such groups:

> 'The trouble for me is not the ones that are involved but the ones that are not. It's always the ones you don't get.'

'The non-active people, the people that won't be coming to the active age groups, how would we contact those? It will be very difficult I would say.'

5.2.2.3 General Attitudes to Older People

Finally, one interviewee felt that attitudes held by people in the CDBs towards older people could be a source of tension:

'[There are] huge tensions around the effectiveness of the consultation and direction of older people's work in the CDB ... very often around attitudes to older people.'

5.3 Interviews with Older People and Older People's Representative Organisations

5.3.1 Views on the Overall Effectiveness of the CDBs

Older people and their representatives were asked for their views on how effective they felt their local CDB was. This question was asked in order to assess the impact of the CDB on older people. There was a spread of opinion in the views of older people's representatives on the overall effectiveness of the CDBs, with a slightly greater number of interviewees having a negative opinion than a positive one. Those who felt that the CDB in their area was effective thought this was particularly the case in the areas of cooperation and networking, consultation, funding and personnel.

Five interviewees said that their CDB had helped to forge good working relationships both within the CDB and across the voluntary/community sector, older people, local development agencies and the health board:

'It has helped to bring all the elderly together to look at areas that might have been left out.'

'We would have had people represented on the CDB from the community and the fact that they were involved in the policies and that type of thing, that has made an impact. We have always had good partnerships down the years.'

One interviewee said that consultation had been an integral part of the relationship between her organisation and the CDB:

'The CDB and the local representatives in [county] have a very good working relationship. Consultation has been a key feature of this relationship. Older people are always consulted and considered to be a priority and they continue to participate in the process.'

One interviewee said that her organisation could not continue to function without the support of the CDB, especially regarding funding.

On the other hand, nine interviewees were dissatisfied with the effectiveness of the CDB. Some of the key reasons put forward for this included:

- communication difficulties between the CDB and the community
- too many meetings and committees
- lack of implementation of CDB strategy
- poor liaison with older people's groups in the community
- CDBs' efforts to organise voluntary groups too restrictive.

Three interviewees said they were not familiar enough with the CDB to assess its effectiveness. One interviewee felt the CDB had only engaged with organised groups of older people and had not been able to access more vulnerable and isolated older people.

5.3.2 Views on Consultation with Older People by CDBs

Interviewees were asked whether they felt older people and their representative organisations were consulted about the work of the CDBs. Twenty-two older people and their representatives gave their opinions on this issue. The majority of these were negative as indicated in Table 5.2.

Table 5.2 Views of older people and their representatives on the levels of consultation carried out by the CDBs

Views of older people	Number of CDBs
Negative views of consultation	14
Positive views of consultation	4
Mixed views of consultation	4
Total	22

5.3.2.1 Negative Views of Consultation

Fourteen of those interviewed had negative views on the levels of consultation undertaken by the CDBs. There was a strong feeling among them that the CDBs did not engage in consultation, or at least that they had not been consulted by the CDB nor had they heard of other people being consulted by the CDB:

'I believe that they [the CDB] have ticked boxes and not really consulted with older people.'

'Plans are presented as a fait accompli.'

A range of other comments were expressed in relation to consultation. An interviewee in one CDB area felt that communications between the various structures of the CDB (SIM, Community and Voluntary Forum, and older people) were very weak and needed to be improved. Another interviewee felt that the needs of older people had not been taken into account when planning consultation sessions:

'They were all in the evening, dangerous and hard to get to.'

Interestingly, two interviewees argued that older people need funding and support in order to engage properly in consultation:

'They have none [input] whatsoever ... what I would like to see is parish councils or even community groups taking some type of funding from CDBs – to be better able to deal with them.'

'There needs to be some kind of way of doing it ... on the community forums you've got the representatives of all the different areas but I think those sectors need to be supported in feeding back ... maybe some funding to get some notes typed up.'

In one CDB area, older people's representatives questioned whether it was necessary to consult older people separately. It should be noted that this was a focus group organised by County Council staff and consisted mainly of local authority, statutory and local development personnel with only two representatives of older people. The reasons given for this were that older people are not a distinct group from the general public and that each older person is different so it is not appropriate to treat them as a homogenous group:

'They're not a different group, I mean, we're all going to be older.'

'They're not homogenous either, they're not all the same ... they're all individuals.'

Finally, in one CDB area, interviews carried out with older people revealed a lack of awareness of the existence of the CDB. However, they strongly felt that the local authority in question did not take account of their needs.

5.3.2.2 Positive Views of Consultation

Four of the older people's representatives interviewed felt that the CDB had made an effort to consult older people. Generally the interviewees were not especially effusive about this; in three of the four CDB areas in question, the interviewees said that some level of consultation had taken place with older people while the CDB strategy was being prepared. In one CDB area, the interviewee gave a more positive response stating that older people were consulted about local plans from the beginning of the work of the CDB and before:

'Oh they would have been involved in local plans all along. From the beginning here, even with regard to building the community centre, the childcare building and other projects, they would have been involved all along.'

'The information loop is very good between the CDB and local players and includes consultation with older people themselves.'

5.3.2.3 Mixed Views of Consultation

Four interviewees had mixed feelings about the consultations with older people undertaken by the CDB. One interviewee did not refer to consultation carried out by the CDB but did say that older people's views are incorporated into all plans for the project she worked on (a sheltered housing project). Another said that while there had not been a specific consultation exercise conducted by the CDB, the Board did link in with existing community systems:

'There wasn't a specific consultation exercise conducted by the SIM, but they linked in with community systems already in place.'

Results from a focus group held with representatives in a third CDB area indicated that they were aware of initial consultation carried out while the CDB strategy was being developed, however they had not received any feedback on progress since that time.

5.3.3 Views on Information Dissemination

The issue of the adequacy of information disseminated by the CDBs was raised in 13 of the interviews. Of these, six interviewees said that the CDB disseminated information either through a newsletter or on request. However, one of the interviewees had some doubts as to the relevance of such information and another referred to a lack of information regarding implementation of the county strategy:

'I know we do have some very very good literature. There is a good CDB plan but there isn't a lot around how it is implemented.'

'[The CDB] will send out information, but how useful this is to older people I don't know.'

Four of those interviewed felt that the CDB did not disseminate information adequately or did not disseminate information at all:

'It is very hard to access useful information about funding and so on.'

'There is no formal information dissemination strategy in place.'

A further three interviewees said they did not know whether the CDB disseminated information or not.

5.3.4 Views on Service Provision for Older People

Of the 22 people interviewed, 17 identified gaps in existing social inclusion activity for older people. A wide range of recommendations were made in this regard. Many recommendations did not fall under the remit of the CDB, but refer to other national and local agencies. For this reason, those recommendations that were deemed to be most relevant to the CDBs and that were identified most frequently were categorised and are summarised in Table 5.3. However, two issues arose that are of special interest to the work of CDBs and SIMs and are therefore discussed in more depth.

Table 5.3 Recommendations to address gaps in existing services for older people

- Provide more accommodation for older people, giving a wide range of good quality options
- Introduce transport initiatives where none exist and extend rural transport initiatives already in place
- Introduce comprehensive domiciliary care services and extend the home help service
- Introduce tailored information dissemination systems for older people
- Tackle the safety and security concerns of older people
- Introduce multi-annual funding for agencies working with older people
- Support and give recognition to voluntary organisations working with older people
- Engage with and access isolated older people
- Introduce dedicated workers for older people

5.3.4.1 Isolated Older People

The issue of how to engage with isolated older people was raised by older people and their representative organisations, as well as by representatives of CDBs and SIMs. Five interviewees discussed this issue in some detail. Isolation of older people posed difficulties in terms of the delivery of services to those who needed them:

> 'We outreach as best we can but you can never touch that lady or gentleman that's living in the country isolated ... they're not on any of our databases.'

Lack of funding and resources also prevented organisations from including this group of older people in their activities:

> 'I'm really concerned about the people out there who are living alone who we're not getting in contact with at all, because they're not going to come out to us ...'

In the main, concerns expressed by older people's representatives reflected those of representatives of CDBs and SIMs. Very isolated older people are at risk of falling through the nets of both statutory agencies and voluntary groups, and the problem of how to include them is yet to be solved.

5.3.4.2 Dedicated Workers for Older People

Dedicated workers for older people were seen as being of significant importance and it was felt that such workers should be put in place as a matter of urgency. Seven interviewees raised this and there was significant consistency across interviews as to the role of such a worker, i.e. to work as a facilitator and development officer in a CDB area dealing solely with older people. He or she should have four main tasks:

■ supporting older people in setting up new active age groups or clubs

■ acting as a liaison between older people and local development agencies (local authorities, NGOs and voluntary organisations, and health services)

■ disseminating information and assisting in funding applications

■ forming contacts with more isolated older people.

Respondents felt that the presence of such a worker would enable older people to organise themselves and strengthen their voice in the community:

' ... some type of a development officer ... that would have a communication with elderly groups, who would actually go and meet elderly groups at some particular point.'

' ... If we had a dedicated worker now there's so much more that could happen.'

'You do need a facilitator to visit each group and assess the needs of each group, and then come back with their needs, or trying to sort out their needs.'

Particulars regarding funding, organisational and employment arrangements for this key worker were not forthcoming in the interviews, possibly because older people were not familiar with the organisational and decision-making processes within local government and did not feel it was within their remit to make these kinds of decisions.

In general, while two in five CDB interviewees stated that they had targeted consultation efforts at older people (most often at the stage of development of CDB strategies or integrated target group plans), the awareness of such efforts was low among the older people and their representatives interviewed. Even among those who were aware of CDB-driven consultation exercises, there were complaints that feedback on progress was poor. This has led to some older people and their representatives feeling alienated from the work of the CDBs and unsure of their purpose. On the other hand, there were more positive views about the effectiveness of the CDBs among those who were familiar with them, indicating that CDBs have the potential to benefit older people if effective feedback and consultation mechanisms are put in place.

This situation is not helped by the barriers perceived by CDB interviewees in attempting to consult with older people. This view was echoed to a certain extent by those older people's representatives who saw a need for dedicated workers for older people to address these barriers. Further research may be necessary to ascertain the extent to which the problems of isolation and lack of organisation impact on the potential for effective consultation, how they can be resolved, and (importantly) whether these barriers reflect an attitudinal or cultural clash between local authorities and older people's organisations.

124

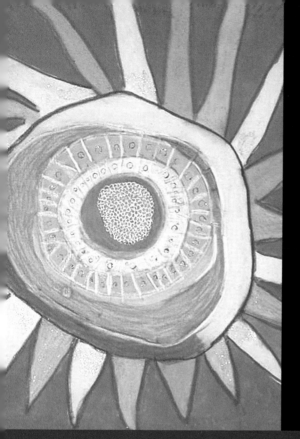

Chapter Six

Conclusions

Chapter Six

Conclusions

6.1 Introduction

This chapter presents the main conclusions that have been drawn from the results of the research. The conclusions and associated recommended actions focus on the following:

- the role and contribution of the CDBs to the social inclusion of older people at local level, and the scope for extension and improvement in this area

- the role and contribution of other local and national agencies to the social inclusion of older people at local level.

This analysis is timely given that the CDBs have been in operation for a number of years. In addition, there have been a number of developments that suggest that this is an opportune time to seek to promote the social inclusion agenda for older people at local level via the CDBs and associated local processes, such as the SIMs and the Community and Voluntary Fora. These will help to put in place mechanisms to improve the consistency of approach to social inclusion issues by the CDBs and SIMs, and to enhance the reach and effectiveness of the Community and Voluntary Fora. They provide a genuine opportunity for ensuring the concerns of older people are placed on the local development agenda.

The recommended actions have been proposed on the basis of the research findings and conclusions. In all cases, such actions should seek to build on existing work of relevance, including work by the NCAOP, Equality Authority and other key agencies.

The CDBs were established to fulfil a central role in local government policy in Ireland. Social inclusion is an important aspect of their remit in relation to economic and social development. In this context, they have the potential to make a significant contribution to the promotion of social inclusion of older people at local level. On the basis of the current study, it can be concluded that while older people's concerns are already on the CDBs' agenda there is room for a significant extension and enhancement of their role and contribution in this regard. Key mechanisms for achieving this include:

- including older people and older people's representative organisations in local level planning and decision-making

- addressing older people's concerns in a comprehensive manner.

6.2.1 Inclusion of Older People in Local Level Planning and Decision-Making

Social inclusion initiatives are as much about the process of decision-making as about tangible outcomes for target groups. Therefore, the involvement of older people should in itself be part of the social inclusion process. In addition, older people themselves are best able to identify their own needs and how they should be met.

The older people's representatives consulted during the course of this study consistently reported the involvement of older people to be a problematic area, with a need to enhance of the involvement of older people's organisations in the CDBs. While some CDBs have already recognised this need, others have not.

In relation to the inclusion of older people in local level planning and decision-making, key issues identified in the research include the need for:

- awareness-raising and promotion of progressive attitudes towards ageing and older people among CDB members

- development of effective consultation mechanisms that reach a wide range of older people, not just those who are currently most active, organised and vocal

- capacity-building among older people and their representatives at local level to enable them to participate and contribute effectively.

> **Recommended Actions**
>
> 1. An awareness-raising programme should be launched to promote positive attitudes towards ageing and older people at local level. This should target the CDBs and their member agencies, as well as those involved in related local structures such as the Community and Voluntary Fora.
>
> 2. The measures recently implemented to develop and reinforce the role of the Community and Voluntary Fora provide an opportunity for a nationwide effort to increase the representation and influence of older people in local development processes across Ireland including to raise awareness of the need to involve older people and their representative organisations and to provide guidance on good practice in consulting and involving older people, taking into account the recommendations of the review of the Community and Voluntary Fora carried out in 2004.
>
> 3. A programme focusing on capacity-building among older people's organisations at local level could be developed with a view to ensuring that they are equipped to avail of the opportunities for participation that are emerging. This might begin on a pilot basis, working with older people and their organisations in one or more local areas. A detailed audit of existing levels of organisation, capacities and extent of involvement in local processes could be carried out, followed by the design and implementation of an intervention to address barriers to effective involvement and influence. Based on the results of the pilot intervention, a wider programme of intervention could then be developed across the country.

6.2.2 Addressing Older People's Concerns in a Comprehensive Manner

As well as involving older people and their organisations, there are two main mechanisms through which the CDBs can promote the social inclusion of older people at local level:

- giving a high priority to older people in the CDB strategy, backed up by a comprehensive range of measures to address older people's concerns and the gaps in service provision identified by older people and their representative organisations

- developing the degree of inter-agency coordination needed to provide joined-up services and supports for older people.

6.2.2.1 Giving a High Priority to Older People and Addressing Their Concerns

One practical way that the CDBs can contribute is by ensuring that older people's concerns are fully reflected in the social and economic development strategies that they develop for their areas and that commitments in the strategies are subsequently followed through in practice. Each CDB published its first strategy in 2002 and the current study found that these did, in fact, include many planned activities that directly address the concerns of older people. The extent to which these activities will ultimately be implemented depends on appropriate follow-through by the CDB member agencies. The tracking software currently being implemented at local and national levels will make it possible to monitor progress in delivering the strategies. However, some CDBs have adopted alternative tracking mechanisms due to the delay in implementing the original project-tracking software. It will be necessary to reconcile the various tracking mechanisms across the country to achieve this goal.

There is considerable diversity across the CDBs both in terms of which themes are being addressed and, within a given theme, the specific aspects that are being addressed. In addition, there are some issues of importance for older people that are not yet being given sufficient attention. For example, the issue of income is not very visible on the local agenda. This may be explained by its prominence at national level. Nevertheless, further action on this theme could be taken at local level. The lack of attention to accessible public places is also noteworthy and there is still a lot to be done to ensure that all towns and cities in Ireland are accessible. It was interesting that gender-related issues appeared on the agenda in a few cases; however, the focus was more on gender-specific needs (e.g. vulnerable older men living alone) than on broader issues of equality between men and women in the older population.

In comparison to the specific themes outlined above, less planned activity was found in the CDB strategies in relation to the broader issues of awareness, attitudes and age-positive practices at local level, themes that have been well articulated and developed at national level. Although some of these issues are being addressed to a certain extent by a number of CDBs, through initiatives focusing on intergenerational relations, there is clearly a lot of scope for local social inclusion processes to do more to promote age-positive attitudes at local level.

Overall, as noted earlier, there is considerable diversity across cities and counties in terms of the main themes that are being addressed and, within a given theme, of the specific issues being addressed under that theme. This diversity may, in part, reflect differences in needs in different local areas. However, it may be also be a result of a lack of a common understanding of the social inclusion concerns of older people and, indeed, a lack of a common definition of social inclusion. For this reason, there is a case to be made for provision of national level guidance to the CDBs on the issues of concern to older people and how these can best be addressed. The work of the Equality Authority in preparing guidelines for equality-proofing the local development processes of the CDBs is a good example of what can be done in relation to national level guidance. This could provide a model for what might be done in relation to guidance for the CDBs on the social inclusion of older people. There may also be scope for further developing the age equality dimension of the existing Equality Authority guidelines.

Recommended Actions

4. It is recommended that guidance documentation be prepared and distributed to the CDBs on the concerns of older people and how these can be addressed at local level. One way to progress this might be to seek to work in the first instance, on a pilot basis, with a limited number of CDBs in order to explore the most appropriate approaches before launching a countrywide initiative. The guidance documentation could delineate the issues that need to be addressed to meet the range of concerns of older people, as well as indicating the ways that the various issues could be addressed at local level. This could include measures addressing at-risk older people, issues that apply across the population (recognition, status, equality/anti-discrimination, socially valued roles etc.) and specific themes that are important for many older people (e.g. health and social services, active retirement, social participation). In this regard, it should be noted that perspectives on social inclusion that focus mainly on income and unemployment dimensions do not always capture other aspects of social inclusion and exclusion that are particularly relevant for older people.

6.2.2.2 Gaps in Service Provision Identified by Older People and Their Representative Organisations

In addition to the lack of focus in CDB strategies on certain issues important to older people, a number of gaps in service provision were identified in interviews carried out with older people's representative organisations. These focused on the need to expand choice, mainstream existing initiatives and improve linkages between discrete services. Examples included joining up rural transport initiatives to provide a more comprehensive service, introducing multi-annual funding to facilitate long-term planning and extending domiciliary care services. It is important to take account of these needs in future planning. The fact that interviewees also recommended the introduction of dedicated workers for older people is of note and should be progressed in consultation with older people and their representative organisations.

> ## Recommended Actions
>
> 5. The gaps in service provision identified by older people's organisations should be noted and actions developed to address these. With regard to dedicated workers for older people, a pilot project utilising international best practice could be developed, in partnership with older people and their representative organisations, to explore the cost implications, responsibilities and job description of such a worker.

6.2.2.3 Inter-Agency Coordination and Joined-Up Services for Older People

In addition to the direct measures proposed in their strategies, the CDBs play a central role in the coordination of services and the activities of their member agencies. This is an ongoing aspect of the operations of the CDBs, as well as being reflected in various ways in the CDB strategy documents.

The current study found that although coordination type measures and approaches addressing issues of relevance for older people were to be found in the majority of CDB strategies, there was considerable diversity in the way that the coordination issue was addressed. In general, there was more emphasis on softer measures in this area, such as raising awareness and putting older people on the agenda, rather than on harder measures to analyse whether gaps in service delivery for older people are arising because of coordination problems.

> ## Recommended Actions
>
> 6. It is recommended that an analysis be carried out of the key inter-agency issues that are most pertinent to the concerns of older people at local level. This would examine whether there are gaps in service provision that arise because of a lack of coordination across organisational boundaries. Transport and education are just two of the areas where there is a need for much greater coordination of services for older people. This should take account of the gaps identified by older people's organisations during the course of the current study.

Although the CDBs have considerable potential for delivering on social inclusion for older people at local level in Ireland, it would be inappropriate to place all of the responsibility for this area on them. Other players at both local and national levels must contribute.

Figure 6.1 presents a schematic view of some of the key national and local agencies and programmes with important roles to play in the delivery of social inclusion for older people at the local level. The diagram illustrates the complexity of linkages between national and local agencies. The sheer number of relationships renders coordination between the various bodies problematic. It also means that different agencies may have different priorities which end up competing against each other. Most importantly, it is unreasonable to expect older people or local groups to navigate the various decision-making pathways at local level in order to influence policy-making in an effective manner.

Figure 6.1 Key actors at national and local level (see Appendix Three for glossary)

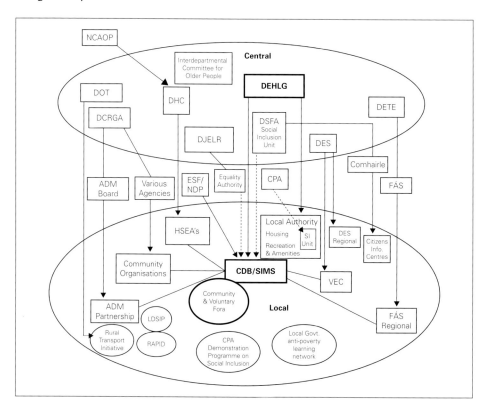

6.3.1 National Level

At national level, the following are key if older people are to be included in social inclusion work at local level:

- inter-Departmental and inter-agency coordination
- measures to ensure a basic level and quality of services for older people in all parts of the country.

6.3.1.1 Inter-Departmental and Inter-Agency Coordination

Reviews of CDB activities and achievements have indicated that many of the inter-agency coordination objectives that have been set for the local level cannot be realised without commensurate inter-Departmental and inter-agency coordination at national level. For this reason, it is necessary to have national level coordination across Government Departments and agencies with roles to play in the social inclusion of older people if a coordinated approach is to be achieved at local level.

Recommended Actions

7. With regard to inter-Departmental and inter-agency coordination at national level, there is a need for a parallel analysis and programme of action to that suggested for local level. This is something that might fall directly within the remit of the Interdepartmental Group on Older People (IDGOP).

6.3.1.2 Ensuring a Basic Level and Quality of Services for Older People

The CDBs were established to provide a locally driven approach to identifying priority local development issues and preparing strategies to address these. Clearly, therefore, principles of subsidiarity must be applied when considering what role should be played at national level in relation to ensuring consistency of approach across the country. Nevertheless, Government Departments and public agencies at national level have a responsibility to ensure a basic level and quality of services for older people in all parts of the country.

On the other hand, of course, in the absence of national standards there is a practical need on the ground to develop services at local level to the best possible levels and standards. The CDBs have an important role to play in this through the promotion of improved coordination among the relevant actors, including partnerships with voluntary organisations in the delivery of community services.

8. With regard to ensuring a basic level and quality of services for older people across the country, various Government Departments and national agencies have roles to play in defining and implementing minimum standards. The DoHC and the HSE, in particular, could address the issue of consistent provision and access to services for older people across the country.

6.3.2 Local Level

As can be seen from Figure 6.1, in addition to the CDBs and their member agencies, there are many local agencies and programmes with roles to play in the delivery of social inclusion measures for older people including:

- programmes related to social inclusion managed by ADM (LDSIP, RAPID and the Rural Transport Initiative)

- community development programmes funded by the DoCRGA

- local level initiatives on social inclusion by the CPA.

Recommended Actions

9. The awareness-raising and guidance activities proposed earlier in this chapter for the CDBs could also be targeted towards these other local level agencies and activities.

References

References

Area Development Management Ltd, 2001. *Local Development Social Inclusion Programme*. Dublin: ADM Ltd.

Brenner, H. and Shelley, E., 1998. *Adding Years to Life and Life to Years: A Health Promotion Strategy for Older People in Ireland*. Dublin: NCAOP.

Burchardt, T., 2000. 'Social exclusion: concepts and evidence' in D. Gordon and P. Townsend (eds) *Breadline Europe: The Measurement of Poverty*. Bristol: Policy Press.

Burchardt, T., Le Grand, J. and Piachaud, D., 1999. 'Social exclusion in Britain 1991-1995', *Social Policy and Administration*, 33: 227-244.

Byrne, D., 1999. *Social Exclusion*. Buckingham: Open University Press.

Combat Poverty Agency, 2004. *Poverty in Ireland – The Facts: 2001. Poverty Briefing 16 – Summer 2004*. Dublin: CPA.

Commission of the European Communities, 1999. *Towards a Europe for All Ages: Promoting Prosperity and Intergenerational Solidarity*. Brussels: Commission of the European Communities.

Commission of the European Communities, 2004. *Communication from the Commission to the Council, the European Parliament, the European Economic and Social Committee and the Committee of the Regions. Modernising Social Protection for the Development of High Quality Accessible and Sustainable Health Care and Long Term Care: Support for the National Strategies Using the 'Open Method of Coordination'*. Brussels: Commission of the European Communities.

Council of the European Union, 2000. *Establishing a General Framework for Equal Treatment in Employment and Occupation*. Brussels: Council of the European Union.

Council of the European Union, 2004. *Joint Report by the Commission and Council on Social Inclusion*. Brussels: Council of the European Union.

Cousins, M., 2003. 'Submissions on NAPSincl 2003-2005' in *Report on Consultation for National Action Plan against Poverty and Social Exclusion 2003-2005*. Dublin: OSI.

Department of the Environment, Heritage and Local Government, 2004. *Improving Local and Community Development Structures and Programmes*. Dublin: DoEHLG.

Department of the Environment, Heritage and Local Government, unpublished. *Review of Community and Voluntary Fora*. Dublin: DoEHLG.

Department of the Taoiseach, 1997. *Partnership 2000*. Dublin: Stationery Office.

Department of the Taoiseach, 2003. *Sustaining Progress: Social Partnership Agreement 2003-2005*. Dublin: Stationery Office.

Fitzpatrick Associates and ERM Ltd, 2003. *Review of County/City Development Board Strategies*. Dublin: DoEHLG.

Government of Ireland, 1997. *Sharing in Progress: National Anti-Poverty Strategy*. Dublin: Stationery Office.

Interdepartmental Task Force on the Integration of Local Government and Local Development, 2000a. *Working Group – Social Inclusion Measures Report*. Dublin: DoEHLG.

Interdepartmental Task Force on the Integration of Local Government and Local Development, 2000b. *A Shared Vision for County/City Development Boards: Guidelines on the CDB Strategies for Economic, Social and Cultural Development*. Dublin: DoEHLG.

Layte, R., Fahey, T. and Whelan, C., 1999. *Income, Deprivation and Well-being among Older Irish People*. Dublin: NCAOP.

Leisering, L. and Walker, R., 1998. *The Dynamics of Modern Society*. Bristol: Policy Press.

Levitas, R., 1998. *The Inclusive Society? Social Exclusion and New Labour*. Basingstoke: Macmillan.

Levitas, R., 2003. 'The idea of social inclusion', paper presented at the 2003 Social Inclusion Research Conference. http://www.ccsd.ca/events/inclusion/papers/rlevitas.htm.

National Council on Ageing and Older People, 2000. *A Framework for Quality in Long-Term Residential Care for Older People in Ireland*. Dublin: NCAOP.

National Council on Ageing and Older People, 2001a. *Submission to the National Anti-Poverty Strategy Working Group on Education*. Dublin: NCAOP.

National Council on Ageing and Older People, 2001b. *Submission to the National Anti-Poverty Strategy Working Group on Employment*. Dublin: NCAOP.

National Council on Ageing and Older People, 2001c. *Submission to the National Anti-Poverty Strategy Working Group on Housing*. Dublin: NCAOP.

National Council on Ageing and Older People, 2001d. *Submission to the National Anti-Poverty Strategy Working Group on Health*. Dublin: NCAÓP.

National Council on Ageing and Older People, 2001e. *Submission to the National Anti-Poverty Strategy Working Group on Rural Disadvantage*. Dublin: NCAOP.

National Council on Ageing and Older People, 2001f. *Submission to the National Anti-Poverty Strategy Working Group on Urban Disadvantage*. Dublin: NCAOP.

National Council on Ageing and Older People, 2005. *An Age Friendly Society: A Position Statement*. Dublin: NCAOP.

National Economic and Social Forum, 2002. *Equality Policies for Older People: Implementation Issues*. Dublin: NESF.

NDP/CSF Evaluation Unit, 1999. *Ex Ante Evaluation of the National Development Plan, 2000-2006*. Dublin: Department of Finance.

NDP/CSF Evaluation Unit, 2003. *Evaluation of Social Inclusion Coordination Mechanisms*. Dublin: Department of Finance.

Office for Social Inclusion, 2003. *National Action Plan against Poverty and Social Exclusion 2003-2005*. Dublin: OSI.

O'Shea, E. and O'Reilly, S., 1999. *An Action Plan for Dementia*. Dublin: NCAOP.

Perri 6, 1997. 'Social inclusion: time to be optimistic', *Demos Collection*, 12: 3-9.

Phillipson, C., 1998. *Reconstructing Old Age*. London: Sage.

Phillipson, C., Bernard, M., Phillips, J. and Ogg, J., 2000. *Family and Community Life of Older People*. London: Routledge.

Phillipson, C. and Scharf, T., 2004. *The Impact of Government Policy on Social Exclusion among Older People: A Review of the Literature for the Social Exclusion Unit Breaking the Cycle Series*. London: Office of the Deputy Prime Minister.

Ruddle, H., Donoghue, F. and Mulvihill, R., 1997. *The Years Ahead Report: A Review of the Implementation of its Recommendations*. Dublin: NCAOP.

Scharf, T., Phillipson, C., Kingston, P. and Smith, A., 2002. 'Social exclusion and older people: exploring the connections', *Education and Ageing* 16, 3: 303-320.

Scharf, T. and Smith, A., 2004. 'Older people in urban neighbourhoods, addressing the risk of social exclusion in later life' in C. Phillipson, G. Allan and D. Morgan (eds) *Social Networks and Social Exclusion*. Aldershot: Ashgate.

The Equality Authority, 2001. *Equality, Poverty and Social Inclusion: The National Action Plan on Social Inclusion. An Equality Authority Position*. Dublin: The Equality Authority.

The Equality Authority, 2002. *Implementing Equality for Older People*. Dublin: The Equality Authority.

United Nations, 2002. *Report of the Second World Assembly on Ageing*. New York: UN.

Wexford Area Partnership, 2000. *Social Inclusion Plan for the Wexford Area 2000-2006*. Wexford: Wexford Area Partnership.

Working Group on Elder Abuse, 2002. *Protecting Our Future: Report of the Working Group on Elder Abuse*. Dublin: Stationery Office.

Working Party on Services for the Elderly, 1988. *The Years Ahead: A Policy for the Elderly*. Dublin: Stationery Office.

Appendices

Appendix One

Interview Schedules

Semi-structured interview schedule for use with SIM groups or other relevant organisations.representatives of CDBs or SIM working groups

1. Introduction and warm up

2. Definitions of social inclusion

    ■   What definitions of social inclusion were used by the CDB in the preparation of the County Strategy?

3. Composition of CDBs

    ■   Validation exercise: current organisation of SIM/relevant body being interviewed

    ■   Are there any other structures/organisational features relevant to social inclusion of older people that we should know about but are missing from the published strategy document?

    ■   Relationship between SIM/relevant body being interviewed and CDB

    ■   How active is SIM/relevant body at the moment

        –   barriers to activity?

        –   opportunities for activity?

4. Prioritising areas for social inclusion measures

    ■   How were priority areas for social inclusion measures **in general** identified?

5. Identification of specific measures that will have an impact on older people directly

    ■   What are the specific social inclusion measures ongoing or planned for older people? (validate from literature where possible)

    ■   Under what key themes are these measures grouped?

        –   health and community services

        –   education

- lifelong learning

- work and retirement

- income

- transport

- housing

- other

■ How were these agreed?

■ What kind of impact do you feel these measures will have on older people? OR How are older people affected by these measures?

■ Are there other dedicated personnel dealing with social inclusion measures ongoing or planned for older people in the SIM/relevant body?

■ Are there any other social inclusion measures that you feel would impact on older people indirectly?

6. Social inclusion projects

■ In your opinion is there any activity(ies) you feel have been successful?

■ If so would you consider this (these) to be an example(s) of good/best practice?

Probe for healthy ageing headings:

- was a needs assessment carried out before start of project?

- were older people consulted about the planning and delivery of the project?

- was participation in the project by older people encouraged?

- how was the project funded?

- has the project been evaluated?

- were all potential categories of older people included in the project?

- how is information about the project disseminated?

■ Are you aware of any other organisations that are dealing with social inclusion measures ongoing or planned for older people outside of SIM/ CDB activity?

7. Methodologies of SIM/relevant body re: older people and how their needs have been identified

- How much input did older people and the organisations that represent them have in the process of identifying social inclusion activities for older people?

- Were older people identified as a distinct group with regard to social inclusion? (validate information from literature where available)

- If so, how were the needs of older people as a distinct group identified?

- If not, how were social inclusion measures for older people incorporated into the strategy and work of the SIM/relevant body?

- Were older people and their organisations that represent them consulted about the work of the CDB? Probe – when did consultation take place, at the planning stage or during the work of the CDB and preparation of the County Strategy?

- Is participation in the work of the CDB encouraged? How?

8. Wind down

Schedule for meetings with representatives of older people

1. Introduction and warm up

2. Measures being planned or undertaken at local level to promote the social inclusion of older people

- Are you aware of any social inclusion projects being planned or currently under way in your area? Probe for

  - title of project

  - name of organisations running the project

  - brief description of project

  - contact details

- If you are, would you consider any of them to be an example of good/best practice? Probe for healthy ageing headings

  - was a needs assessment carried out?

  - were older people consulted about the planning and delivery of the project?

       –   was participation in the project by older people encouraged?

       –   how was the project funded?

       –   has the project been evaluated?

       –   were all potential categories of older people included in the project?

       –   how was information about the project disseminated?

3.   The effectiveness of the CDB in promoting social exclusion

    ■   How effective do you feel the local CDB has been in the promotion of social inclusion for older people?

4.   Ascertaining the degree of input of older people and the organisations that represent them into the social inclusion work of the CDBs

    ■   Are older people and the organisations that represent them consulted about the work of the CDB?

    ■   Do you feel that the needs of users and providers have been considered in the planning of the county strategy and allied documentation?

    ■   Does the CDB disseminate information to the community? Probe:

       –   regularly or irregularly?

       –   accessible?

       –   easy to understand?

5.   Identification of gaps in existing social inclusion measures and the additional measures required to facilitate greater inclusion and participation by older people in the CDBs and in Irish society.

    ■   Can you think of any areas important to older people that are not currently addressed by existing social inclusion measures?

Appendix Two

Examples of Social Inclusion Activities

Charleville Sheltered Housing Services

Charleville Sheltered Housing Services is a company limited by share capital. The DoEHLG provided 90 per cent of building costs. In addition, the company engaged in fundraising events. These have been supported by the local community and people in the wider catchment area. The company provides sheltered housing through individual accommodation units in a residential village setting. It is available to any income or age category. Each accommodation unit consists of a living room, kitchenette and bedroom with bathroom en-suite. A four-course lunch is provided in the central care dining room six days a week (excluding Sundays and bank holidays). In addition, residents can have lunch delivered to their houses when necessary.

A staff rota provides general and personal care between 9 a.m. and 7 p.m. Outside these hours, there is a telephone/beeper system that operates on call, along with a nurse manager who attends to medical needs on site.

Contracts of care are drawn up that outline the company's obligations and those of the resident. In addition, the company is audited annually on a statutory basis. Residents pay a weekly charge of €90.00 and retain their pension.

There is also a group house providing individual accommodation for four people, offering full board and enhanced care supports seven days a week. This accommodation costs €200 per week.

The CHOICE Programme in the North-West

This is a project that aims to follow the principles of respect, dignity and choice, person-centred care, holistic care and needs-driven care. The project aims to create a system of care based on the choices of older people and which responds to their lifetime opportunities and needs.

The three main objectives of the CHOICE programme are to:

- work with older people in developing services that will respond to their lifetime opportunities, needs and choices

- support older people in healthy ageing and maintain and develop services to enable the older person to remain at home for as long as possible

- maintain and develop home-like residential services for those who can no longer remain at home, in line with the principles of CHOICE.

A number of actions have been taken to date, including:

- awareness-raising activities such as the production of a video for information dissemination among healthcare professionals, older people and the general public

- focus groups with older people in the target counties

- workshops with older people and health professionals

- a survey of older people's needs and wants in Co. Donegal.

However, delays in rolling out the Primary Care Strategy and associated funding has hampered full implementation of the CHOICE programme as it was first conceived, leading to disappointment among community groups and representative organisations for older people in the target counties.

Planning Health Services for Older People – Co. Limerick CDB

This initiative aims to support community groups to research older people's needs and apply to the HSE Mid-Western Region for the Older People's Services Grant. It is to be carried out by the Community Council in Co. Limerick, with the CDB ready to lend support if required. As part of this project, the Community Council are to set up their own sub-committee which will involve the senior citizens' committee to assess needs and apply for funding.

Health Board Literacy Proofing – Co. Offaly CDB

Past experience and feedback from PHNs in Co. Offaly indicated that many older people could not read the health information leaflets handed out by nurses. After discussions between the CDB and the then Midland Health Board (MHB), the health service has started to make their key documents more accessible to people with literacy problems and this process is expected to continue.

Safety at Home for Older People – Western Health Board/Co. Mayo

Hip protectors are light cast plastic protectors designed to fit on the hips and protect the wearer from fracture if they fall. In conjunction with the occupational therapist, physiotherapist and director of nursing in a day care centre in Westport, eight older people attending day care will receive hip protectors in an effort to reduce their risk of injury.

IT Training for Older People – Ballinasloe Community Resources

Ballinasloe Community Resources run introductory ICT courses for older people on Tuesdays and Thursdays, with three CE workers providing tuition in basic ICT skills. There is no fixed length to each session and course content is tailored to the needs and progress of the students involved. Likewise, course length is not fixed and varies according to students' circumstances. There is no charge for the course. There has been significant demand for places and feedback from participants has been very positive. Three important factors that have encouraged older people to attend are a friendly atmosphere, an unstructured teaching environment and a low pupil to teacher ratio.

Go for Life and PALs

The Go For Life programme is a national programme for sport and physical activity for older people. It is an Age and Opportunity initiative funded by the Irish Sports Council. The aim of the programme is to empower and enable older people by reaching out to ARAs, senior citizens' groups, day care and community centres across the country. There are four elements to the programme: an active living programme; a sports participation programme; a national grants scheme; and newsletters, fact sheets and information. As such, it can be seen to straddle both health and sports sectors.

PALs is one strand of the Go For Life programme and consists of a series of workshops to enable the participants to plan and lead health-enhancing physical activity sessions for older people. These workshops aim to enable the participants to plan and lead health-enhancing physical activity sessions for older people. The workshops are a combination of theory and practical ideas. Each workshop is approximately five hours long and the series of workshops are organised over a number of weeks in a given area at local level.

The Rural Transport Initiative

The Rural Transport Initiative (RTI) arose from a commitment by the Department of Transport in the NDP, where a provision for up to €4.4 million was earmarked to support the development of pilot public transport initiatives in rural areas. The initiative was launched in 2001 following a consultation process and 34 projects are currently participating. ADM Ltd manages the initiative on behalf of the Department of Transport with the funding coming from the Department.

In the view of many interviewees, the RTI has had a huge impact on the lives of older people who can access it. This was especially evident from interviews carried out with older people or their representative organisations. The most popular aspect of the transport initiatives was the opportunity for social contact between older people.

Appendix Three

Glossary of Terms for Figure 6.1

ADM Area Development Management Limited is an intermediary company operating under company law. It was established by the Irish Government in agreement with the European Union to promote social inclusion, reconciliation and equality and to counter disadvantage through local social and economic development.

Comhairle The national agency responsible for supporting the provision of information, advice and advocacy on social services. It supports a network of Citizen's Information Centres (CICs) in about 100 locations around Ireland.

CPA Combat Poverty Agency. The national statutory agency dedicated to advising on ways to prevent and eliminate poverty and social exclusion.

DoCRGA Department of Community, Rural and Gaeltacht Affairs

DoEHLG Department of Environment, Heritage and Local Government

DoETE Department of Enterprise, Trade and Industry

DoES Department of Education and Science

DoHC Department of Health and Children

DoJELR Department of Justice, Equality and Law Reform

DoT Department of Transport

DoSFA Department of Social and Family Affairs

Equality Authority The Equality Authority is the national agency responsible for ensuring that all citizens in the country are treated equally and to ensure that discrimination on certain grounds does not occur.

FÁS The training and employment authority. It was established in 1988 under the Labour Services Act, 1987. Key functions include training and retraining, designated apprenticeships, recruitment services, employment schemes, placement and guidance services, assistance for community groups, advice for people returning to Ireland and those seeking employment elsewhere in the EU. It also provides consultancy and HR related services on a commercial basis outside the State, and engages in the collection and publication of information relating to the labour market.

HSEAs Health Service Executive Areas. The Health Service Executive assumed responsibility for the health service in the Republic of Ireland on 1 January 2005. The functions of the pre-existing regional health boards have now transferred to the HSE. The older health boards are now known as Areas.

LDSIP The Local Development Social Inclusion Programme. Consists of a series of measures designed to counter disadvantage and to promote equality and social and economic inclusion.

NDP/CSF National Development Plan/Community Support Framework Evaluation Unit. The key body involved in evaluation of the National Development Plan (NDP) and Community Support Framework (CSF) for Ireland 2000-2006. The unit is an independent unit under the aegis of the Department of Finance.

RAPID Revitalising Areas by Planning, Investment and Development is a focused Government initiative to target the 45 most disadvantaged urban areas and provincial towns in the country.

VECs VECs are local level statutory education and training authorities, established under the Vocational Education Act, 1930.

150

Terms of
Reference

Terms of Reference

The National Council on Ageing and Older People was established on 19th March 1997 in succession to the National Council for the Elderly (January 1990 to March 1997) and the National Council for the Aged (June 1981 to January 1990).

The functions of the Council are as follows:

1. To advise the Minister for Health on all aspects of ageing and the welfare of older people, either at its own initiative or at the request of the Minister and in particular on:

   a) measures to promote the health of older people;

   b) measures to promote the social inclusion of older people;

   c) the implementation of the recommendations contained in policy reports commissioned by the Minister for Health;

   d) methods of ensuring co-ordination between public bodies at national and local level in the planning and provision of services for older people;

   e) methods of encouraging greater partnership between statutory and voluntary bodies in providing services for older people;

   f) meeting the needs of the most vulnerable older people;

   g) means of encouraging positive attitudes to life after 65 years and the process of ageing;

   h) means of encouraging greater participation by older people;

   i) whatever action, based on research, is required to plan and develop services for older people.

2. To assist the development of national and regional policies and strategies designed to produce health gain and social gain for older people by:

    a) undertaking research on the lifestyle and the needs of older people in Ireland;

    b) identifying and promoting models of good practice in the care of older people and service delivery to them;

    c) providing information and advice based on research findings to those involved in the development and/or implementation of policies and services pertaining to the health, well-being and autonomy of older people;

    d) liaising with statutory, voluntary and professional bodies involved in the development and/or implementation of national and regional policies which have as their object health gain or social gain for older people.

3. To promote the health, welfare and autonomy of older people.

4. To promote a better understanding of ageing and older people in Ireland.

5. To liaise with international bodies which have functions similar to the functions of the Council.

The Council may also advise other Ministers, at their request, on aspects of ageing and the welfare of older people which are within the functions of the Council.

Membership

Chairperson Cllr Éibhlin Byrne

Mr Bernard Thompson

Mr Eddie Wade

Mr Michael Dineen

Fr Peter Finnerty

Mr Eamon Kane

Mr Michael Murphy

Mr Pat O'Toole

Ms Pauline Clancy-Seymour

Mr Noel Byrne

Dr Davida de la Harpe

Dr Ruth Loane

Mr Paddy O'Brien

Ms Bernard Thompson

Ms Annette Kelly

Mr Paul O'Donoghue

Ms Mary O'Neill

Cllr Jim Cousins

Dr Ciaran Donegan

Mr James Flanagan

Dr Michael Loftus

Ms Mary Nally

Ms Rosemary Smith

Mr John Brady

Ms Kit Carolan

Mr John Grant

Ms Sylvia Meehan

Ms Martina Queally

Mr Oliver R Cleary

Ms Eileen O'Dolan

Ms Elaine Soffe

Director Bob Carroll

156